POPE FRANCIS

Against War

Building a Culture of Peace

T0054494

POPE FRANCIS

Against War

Building a Culture of Peace

With an Afterword by Andrea Tornielli

ORBIS BOOKS
www.orbisbooks.com

ORBIS BOOKS
www.orbisbooks.com

Fathers and Brothers
MARYKNOLL.

Founded in 1970, Orbis Books endeavors to publish works that enlighten the mind, nourish the spirit, and challenge the conscience. The publishing arm of the Maryknoll Fathers and Brothers, Orbis seeks to explore the global dimensions of the Christian faith and mission, to invite dialogue with diverse cultures and religious traditions, and to serve the cause of reconciliation and peace. The books published reflect the views of their authors and do not represent the official position of the Maryknoll Society. To learn more about Maryknoll and Orbis Books, please visit our website at www.orbisbooks.com.

Library of Congress Control Number: 2022939137

Contents

Introduction

War Is a Sacrilege. Let's Stop Feeding It!

A year ago, on my pilgrimage to tormented Iraq, I was able to see for myself the disaster caused by war, fratricidal violence, and terrorism; I saw the rubble of houses and the wounded hearts, but I also saw seeds of hope for rebirth. I would never have imagined then that a year later a conflict would break out in Europe.

From the beginning of my service as bishop of Rome, I have talked about the Third World War, saying that we are already living it, though still in pieces. Those pieces have become bigger and bigger, welding together. . . . So many wars are going on in the world right now, causing immense pain for innocent victims, especially children—wars that cause the flight of millions of people, forced to leave their land, their homes, their devastated cities, to save their own lives. These are the many forgotten wars that reappear from time to time before our disenchanted eyes. These wars often seemed "far away"—until now, suddenly, when war has broken out so close to us. Ukraine was attacked and invaded. Many innocent civilians, women, children, and elderly people have been affected by the conflict, forced to live in shelters dug out of the earth to escape the bombs. Families have been divided as husbands, fathers, and grandparents remain in the fight, while wives, mothers, and grandmothers seek refuge after long journeys, hoping to cross the border to find shelter in other countries that receive them with open hearts.

As every day we face heartbreaking images and hear the cry of children and women, we can only scream, "Stop!" War is not the solution. War is madness, war is a monster, war is a cancer that feeds on itself, engulfing everything! What is more, war is a sacrilege that wreaks havoc on what is most precious on our earth: human life, the innocence of the little ones, the beauty of creation. Yes, war is a sacrilege! I cannot fail to recall the plea with which Saint John XXIII in 1962 asked the leaders of his time to halt an escalation that could have dragged the world into the abyss of nuclear conflict. I cannot forget the force with which Saint Paul VI, speaking in 1965 at the United Nations General Assembly, said, "Never again war! Never again war!" Nor can I forget the many appeals for peace made by Saint John Paul II, who in 1991 described war as "an adventure without return."

What we are witnessing is yet another barbarity and unfortunately we have a short memory. Yes, because if we had a memory, we would remember what our grandparents and our parents told us, and we would feel the need for peace just as our lungs need oxygen. If we had memory, we would not spend tens and hundreds of billions of dollars for rearmament, equipping ourselves with increasingly sophisticated armaments, increasing the market and the trafficking of weapons that end up killing children, women, and old people: $1.981 trillion per year, according to the calculations of an important research center in Stockholm. That marks a dramatic increase of 2.6 percent in military spending in the second year of the pandemic, when all our efforts should have been focused on global health and saving lives from the virus. If we had memory, we would know that war, before it reaches the front lines, must be stopped in the heart. Hate, before it is too late, must be eradicated from hearts. And in order to do so, there is a need for dialogue, negotiation, listening, diplomatic skills and creativity, and farsighted politics capable of building a new system of coexistence that is no longer based on the power of weapons, but on deterrence. Every war is not only a defeat of politics but also a shameful surrender to the forces of evil.

In November 2019, in Hiroshima, a symbolic city whose inhabitants, along with those of Nagasaki, were slaughtered during the Second World War by two nuclear bombs, I reaffirmed that the use of atomic energy for the purposes of war is, today more than ever, a crime, not only against man and his dignity, but against any possibility of a future in our common home. The use of atomic energy for purposes of war is immoral, just as the possession of atomic weapons is immoral.

Who could have imagined that less than three years later the specter of a nuclear war would loom over Europe? So, step by step, we are moving toward catastrophe. Piece by piece the world risks becoming the scene of a unique Third World War. We are moving toward it as if it were inevitable.

Instead, we must forcefully repeat: No, it is not inevitable! No, war is not inescapable! When we allow ourselves to be devoured by this monster represented by war, when we allow this monster to raise its head and guide our actions, we lose everything, we destroy God's creation, we commit sacrilege and prepare a future of death for our children and grandchildren.

Greed, intolerance, ambition for power, and violence are motives that push forward the decision for war, and these motives are often justified by a war ideology that forgets the immeasurable dignity of human life, of every human life, and the respect and care we owe them.

Faced with the images of death that come to us from Ukraine, it is difficult to hope. Yet there are seeds of hope. There are millions of people who do not aspire to war, who do not justify war, but are asking for peace. There are millions of young people who are asking us to do everything possible and seemingly impossible to stop the war, to stop all wars. It is in thinking first of all of them, of young people and children, that we must repeat together: Never again war! And together we must commit ourselves to building a world that is more peaceful because it is more just, where it is peace that triumphs and not the folly of war; justice, and not the injustice of war; mutual forgiveness, and not the hatred that divides and makes us see the other, the person who is different from us, as an enemy.

Here I would like to quote an Italian pastor of souls, the venerable Don Tonino Bello, bishop of Molfetta-Ruvo-Giovinazzo-Terlizzi, in Puglia, a tireless prophet of peace, who loved to repeat: conflicts and all wars "find their root in the fading away of faces." When we erase the face of the other, then the noise of weapons crackles. When we keep the other person, his or her face and pain, before our eyes, then we are not allowed to violently disfigure his or her dignity.

In my encyclical *Fratelli tutti* I proposed that the money spent on arms and other military expenditures be used to set up a World Fund to finally eliminate hunger and to foster the development of the poorest countries, so that their inhabitants would not resort to violent or deceptive solutions and would not be forced to leave their countries in search of a more dignified life.

I renew this proposal today, especially today. Because war must be stopped, all wars must be stopped, and they will only stop if we stop "feeding" them.

From the Vatican
March 29, 2022

Francesco

With War, No One Wins

War Destroys the Future

Dear brothers and sisters, more than a month has gone by since the beginning of the invasion of Ukraine, since the beginning of this cruel and senseless war, that, like every war, represents a defeat for everyone, for every one of us. We need to reject war, a place of death where fathers and mothers bury their children, where men kill their brothers and sisters without even having seen them, where the powerful decide and the poor die.

War does not devastate the present only, but the future of a society as well. I read that from the beginning of the aggression in Ukraine, one out of every two children have been displaced from their country. This means destroying the future, causing dramatic trauma in the lives of the smallest and most innocent among us. This is the brutality of war—a barbaric and sacrilegious act!

War should not be something that is inevitable. We should not accustom ourselves to war. Instead, we need to convert today's indignation into tomorrow's commitment, because if we emerge from these events the way we were before, we will all be guilty in some way. Faced with the danger of self-destruction, may humanity understand that the moment has come to abolish war, to erase it from human history, before it erases humans from history.

I pray that every political leader may reflect on this, to commit themselves to this! And, looking on martyred Ukraine, to understand how each day of war worsens the situation for everyone. Therefore, I renew my appeal: Enough. Stop. May weapons be silenced. May peace be seriously pursued. Let us continue to pray untiringly to the Queen of Peace, to whom we consecrated humanity, in particular Russia and Ukraine, with such a huge and intense participation for which I thank all of you.

Angelus
March 27, 2022

We Have Accumulated Weapons and Lost the Peace

We have strayed from that path of peace. We have forgotten the lesson learned from the tragedies of the last century, the sacrifice of the millions who fell in two world wars. We have disregarded the commitments we made as a community of nations. We have betrayed peoples' dreams of peace and the hopes of the young. We grew sick with greed, we thought only of our own nations and their interests, we grew indifferent and caught up in our selfish needs and concerns. We chose to ignore God, to be satisfied with our illusions, to grow arrogant and aggressive, to suppress innocent lives and to stockpile weapons. We stopped being our neighbor's keepers and stewards of our common home. We have ravaged the garden of the earth with war and by our sins we have broken the heart of our heavenly Father, who desires us to be brothers and sisters. We grew indifferent to everyone and everything except ourselves. Now with shame we cry out: Forgive us, Lord!

> *Act of Consecration to the Immaculate Heart of Mary*
> *March 25, 2022*

What's the Point of Showing Your Teeth?

It is now evident that good politics cannot come from the culture of power understood as domination and oppression, but only from a culture of care, care for the person and his or her dignity, and care for our common home. This is proven, unfortunately negatively, by the shameful war we are witnessing. I think that for those of you who belong to my generation it is unbearable to see what has happened and is happening in Ukraine. But unfortunately this is the fruit of the old logic of power that still dominates the so-called geopolitics. The history of the last seventy years shows that there has been no lack of regional wars; that's why I said that we were in the Third World War in bits and pieces, all over the world, until we got to this one, which has a bigger dimension and threatens the whole world. But the basic problem is the same: the world continues to be governed as a "chessboard," where the powerful study the moves to extend their dominance to the detriment of others.

The real answer is not more weapons, more sanctions. I was ashamed when I read that a group of states has pledged to spend 2 percent, I believe, of their GDP on arms purchases, as a response to what is happening now. Madness! The real answer, as I said, is not more weapons, more sanctions, more political-military alliances, but a different approach, a different way to govern the world, now globalized—not by showing teeth, as now—but a different way to set up international relations. The model of care is already in place, thank God, but unfortunately it is still subservient to that of economic-technocratic-military power.

Address to meeting sponsored
by the Italian Women's Center
Sala Clementina
March 24, 2022

With War, No One Wins

The news of displaced persons, of people fleeing, killed, wounded, of so many soldiers fallen on both sides, is news of death. Let us ask the Lord of life to deliver us from this death of war. With war everything is lost, everything. There is no victory in a war; everything is defeated. May the Lord send his Spirit to make us understand that war is a defeat of humanity, to make us understand that instead we need to defeat war. May the Spirit of the Lord free us all from this self-destructive need that is manifested in waging war. Let us also pray that leaders may understand that buying and making weapons is not the solution to the problem. The solution is to work together for peace and, as the Bible says, to turn weapons into instruments for peace.

General Audience
Paul VI Hall
March 23, 2022

Spending on Weapons Sullies the Soul

Why, then, wage war on each other over conflicts that we should resolve by talking to each other as fellow people? Why not rather join our forces and resources to fight together the real battles of civilization: the fight against hunger and thirst, the fight against disease and epidemics, the fight against today's poverty and slavery? Why? Certain choices are not neutral: to allocate a large part of spending to weapons means taking it away from something else, which means continuing to take it away yet again, from those who lack the basic necessities. And this is a scandal: spending on weapons. How much is spent on weapons, terrible! I don't know the exact figure, but it's a high percentage. And we spend on arms in order to wage wars, not only this one, which is very serious, and that we are experiencing now. We feel it more because it is closer, but there are continuous wars in Africa, in the Middle East, in Asia. This is serious. We need to create the awareness that continuing to spend on weapons sullies the soul, sullies the heart, sullies humanity. What is the use of solemnly committing ourselves all together, on an international level, in campaigns against poverty, against hunger, against the degradation of the planet, if we then fall back into the old vice of war, into the old strategy of the power of armaments, which takes everything and everyone backward? A war always takes you backward, always. We walk backward. We will have to start over again.

Greeting to members of I Was Thirsty
(volunteer organization)
Clementine Hall
March 21, 2022

Human Life before Any Strategy

Unfortunately, the violent aggression against Ukraine has not stopped, a senseless massacre where slaughter and atrocities are repeated every day. There is no justification for this! I plead with all those who are involved in the international community to truly be committed to putting an end to this abhorrent war.

Again this week, missiles and bombs have fallen on civilians, the elderly, children, and pregnant mothers. I went to see the wounded children who are here in Rome. One was missing an arm; another had a head injury ... innocent children. I think of the millions of Ukrainian refugees who have to flee, leaving everything behind, and I feel a great pain for those who do not even have the opportunity to escape. Many grandparents, sick and poor people separated from their own families. Many children and fragile people are left to die under the bombs, without being able to receive help and without finding safety even in the air raid shelters. All this is inhuman! Indeed, it is also sacrilegious because it goes against the sacredness of human life, especially against defenseless human life, which should be respected and protected, not eliminated, and which comes before any strategy! Let us not forget, it is inhuman and sacrilegious cruelty! Let us pray in silence for those who are suffering.

It comforts me to know that the people left under the bombs do not lack the closeness of their pastors, who in these tragic days are living the Gospel of charity and fraternity. I have spoken with some of them on the phone during these days. They are close to the people of God. Thank you, dear brothers and sisters, for this witness and for the concrete support you are offering courageously to so many desperate people! I also think of the Apostolic Nuncio, who was just made a Nuncio, Archbishop Visvaldas Kulbokas, who has remained in Kyiv since the beginning of the war along with his collaborators and who with his presence brings me close every day to the martyred Ukrainian people. Let us be close to this people, let us embrace them with affection, with concrete commitment and prayer. And please, let us not get used to war and violence! Let us not tire of welcoming [refugees] with generosity as is being done, not only now during the emergency, but also in the weeks and months to come. Because you know that at first, we all do everything we can to welcome them, but then with habit our hearts are somewhat cooled and we forget. Let us think of these women and children who in time, without work, separated from their husbands, will be sought out by the "vultures" of society. Please, let us protect them.

I invite every community and all the faithful to join me on Friday, March 25, Solemnity of the Annunciation, for the Solemn Act of Consecration of humanity, especially Russia and Ukraine, to the Immaculate Heart of Mary, so that she, the Queen of Peace, may bring peace to the world.

Angelus
March 20, 2022

Abuse of Power Condemns the Helpless

What we have been experiencing in recent weeks is not what we had hoped for after the difficult health emergency caused by the pandemic, which made us experience a sign of powerlessness and fear, together with the fragile condition of our existence. The tragedy of the war that is taking place in the heart of Europe leaves us astonished; we never thought we would see such scenes again, reminiscent of the great wars of the last century. The heartbreaking cry for help from our Ukrainian brothers and sisters urges us as a community of believers not only to reflect seriously, but to cry with them and to do something for them—to share the anguish of a people whose identity, history, and tradition have been wounded. The blood and tears of children, the suffering of women and men who are defending their land or fleeing from bombs rattle our conscience.

Once again humanity is threatened by a perverse abuse of power and partisan interests, which condemns defenseless people to suffer all forms of brutal violence. . . .

Today more than ever it is urgent to review the style and effectiveness of the *ars politica*. In the face of the many changes we are witnessing at an international level, it is our duty to make possible "the development of a global community of fraternity based on the practice of social friendship on the part of peoples and nations" (*Fratelli tutti*, 154). War, which "leaves our world worse than it was before" and is "a failure of politics and of humanity, a shameful capitulation . . . before the forces of evil" (261), may in this sense provoke an opposite reaction, a commitment to reestablish an architecture of peace at the global level (see 231), in which the European house, born to guarantee peace after the world wars, has a primary role.

> *Message on occasion of opening of*
> *European Catholic Social Days*
> *Bratislava*
> *March 15, 2022*

Every Conflict Is a Defeat of Humanity

We are used to hearing news of wars, but far away: Syria, Yemen . . . the usual. Now the war has come closer, it is practically on our doorstep. And this makes us think about the "savagery" of human nature, how far we are capable of going. Murderers of our brothers. Thank you,

Monsignor Guy-Réal Thivierge, for this letter that you brought, which is a wake-up call. It draws attention to what is happening. We talk about education, and when one thinks of education one thinks of children, young people. . . . Let us think of so many soldiers who are sent to the front, very young Russian soldiers, poor things. Think of the many young Ukrainian soldiers; think of the inhabitants, the young people, the boys and girls. . . . This is happening close to us. The Gospel only asks us not to look the other way, which is precisely the most pagan attitude of Christians: when Christians become used to looking the other way, they slowly become pagans disguised as Christians. This is why I wanted to begin with this, with this reflection. The war is not far away: it is on our doorstep. What am I doing? Here in Rome, at the Bambino Gesù Hospital, there are children wounded by the bombings. At home, they take them home. Do I pray? Do I fast? Do I do penance? Or do I live carefree, as we normally live through distant wars? A war is always—always!—the defeat of humanity, always. We, the educated, who work in education, are defeated by this war, because [it is] "elsewhere"; we are responsible. There is no such thing as a just war: they do not exist!

Speech to meeting promoted
by the Gravissium Educationis foundation
Clementine Hall
March 18, 2022

The Good Sense to Negotiate

Rivers of blood and tears are flowing in Ukraine. It is not merely a military operation, but a war that sows death, destruction, and misery. The number of victims is increasing, as are the people fleeing, especially mothers and children. The need for humanitarian assistance in that troubled country is growing dramatically by the hour.

I make a heartfelt appeal for humanitarian corridors to be genuinely secured, and for access to the besieged areas to be guaranteed and facilitated, in order to offer vital relief to our brothers and sisters oppressed by bombs and fear.

I thank all those who are taking in refugees. Above all, I implore that the armed attacks cease and that negotiation—and common sense—prevail. And that international law be respected once again!

And I would also like to thank the journalists who put their lives at risk to guarantee information. Thank you, brothers and sisters, for this service! A service that allows us to be close to the tragedy of that population and enables us to assess the cruelty of a war. Thank you, brothers and sisters.

Let us pray together for Ukraine: here in the front are its flags. Let us pray together, as brothers and sisters, to Our Lady, Queen of Ukraine. Hail Mary. . . .

The Holy See is prepared to do everything to put itself at the service of this peace. In these days, two cardinals went to Ukraine to serve the people, to help. Cardinal Konrad

Krajewski, the almoner, to bring aid to the needy, and Cardinal Michael Czerny, interim prefect of the Dicastery for Promoting Integral Human Development. The presence of the two cardinals there is the presence, not only of the pope, but of all Christian people who want to draw closer and say, "War is madness! Stop, please! Look at this cruelty!"

Angelus
March 6, 2022

Let's Not Forget the Many Wars around the World!

In recent days we have been shaken by something tragic: war. Several times we have prayed that this road would not be taken. And let us not stop praying; indeed, let us implore God more intensely. For this reason, I renew to all the invitation to make March 2, Ash Wednesday, a day of prayer and fasting for peace in Ukraine. A day to be close to the sufferings of the Ukrainian people, to feel that we are all brothers and sisters, and to implore God for the end of the war.

Those who wage war, those who provoke war, forget humanity. They do not start from the people, they do not look at the real life of people, but place partisan interests and power before all else. They trust in the diabolical and perverse logic of weapons, which is furthest from the will of God. And they distance themselves from ordinary people, who want peace, and who are the real victims in every conflict, who pay for the follies of war with their own skin. I think of the elderly, of those who are seeking refuge in these hours, of mothers fleeing with their children. . . . They are brothers and sisters for whom it is urgent to open humanitarian corridors, and who should be welcomed.

With a heart broken by what is happening in Ukraine—and let us not forget the wars in other parts of the world, such as in Yemen, in Syria, in Ethiopia . . .—I repeat: Silence all weapons! God is with the peacemakers, not with those who use violence. Because those who love peace, as the Italian Constitution states, reject "war as an instrument of aggression against the freedom of other peoples and as a means for the settlement of international disputes."

Angelus
February 27, 2022

Those Who Have Weapons Sooner or Later End Up Using Them

Dialogue and fraternity are two essential focal points in our efforts to overcome the crisis of the present moment. Yet "despite numerous efforts aimed at constructive dialogue between nations, the deafening noise of war and conflict is intensifying" [*Message for the 2022 World Day of Peace*, 1]. The entire international community must address the urgent need to find solutions to endless conflicts that at times appear as true proxy wars.

I think first of Syria, where the country's rebirth does not yet clearly appear on the horizon. Even today, the Syrian people mourn their dead and the loss of everything, and continue to hope for a better future. Political and constitutional reforms are required for the country to be reborn, but the imposition of sanctions should not strike directly at everyday life, in order to provide a glimmer of hope to the general populace, increasingly caught in the grip of poverty.

Nor can we overlook the conflict in Yemen, a human tragedy that has gone on for years, silently, far from the spotlight of the media and with a certain indifference on the part of the international community, even as it continues to claim numerous civil victims, particularly women and children.

In the past year, no steps forward were made in the peace process between Israel and Palestine. I would truly like to see these two peoples rebuild mutual trust and resume speaking directly to each other, in order to reach the point where they can live in two states, side by side, in peace and security, without hatred and resentment, but the healing born of mutual forgiveness.

Other sources of concern are the institutional tensions in Libya, the episodes of violence by international terrorism in the Sahel region, and the internal conflicts in Sudan, South Sudan, and Ethiopia, where there is need "to find once again the path of reconciliation and peace through a forthright encounter that places the needs of the people above all else" [*Urbi et Orbi*, December 25, 2021].

Profound situations of inequality and injustice, endemic corruption, and various forms of poverty that offend the dignity of persons also continue to fuel social conflicts on the American continent, where growing polarization is not helping to resolve the real and pressing problems of its people, especially those who are most poor and vulnerable.

Reciprocal trust and readiness to engage in calm discussion should also inspire all parties at stake, so that acceptable and lasting solutions can be found in Ukraine and in the southern Caucasus, and the outbreak of new crises can be avoided in the Balkans, primarily in Bosnia and Herzegovina.

Dialogue and fraternity are all the more urgently needed for dealing wisely and effectively with the crisis that for almost a year now has affected Myanmar; its streets, once places of encounter, are now the scene of fighting that does not spare even houses of prayer.

Naturally, these conflicts are exacerbated by the abundance of weapons on hand and the unscrupulousness of those who make every effort to supply them. At times, we deceive ourselves into thinking that these weapons serve to dissuade potential aggressors. History and, sadly, even daily news reports make it clear that this is not the case. Those who possess weapons will eventually use them, since, as Saint Paul VI observed, "a person cannot love with offensive weapons in his hands" [*Address to the UN*, October 4, 1965]. Furthermore, "When we yield to the logic of arms and distance ourselves from the practice of dialogue, we forget to our detriment that, even before

causing victims and ruination, weapons can create nightmares" [Meeting for Peace, Hiroshima, November 24,
2019]. Today these concerns have become even more real,
if we consider the availability and employment of auton-
omous weapon systems that can have terrible and unforeseen consequences, and should be subject to the responsibility of the international community.

Among the weapons humanity has produced, nuclear
arms are of particular concern. At the end of last December, the Tenth Review Conference of the parties to the
Treaty on the Non-Proliferation of Nuclear Weapons,
which was to meet in New York, was once again post-
poned due to the pandemic. A world free of nuclear arms
is possible and necessary. I therefore express my hope that
the international community will view that conference as
an opportunity to take a significant step in this direction.
The Holy See continues steadfastly to maintain that in
the twenty-first century nuclear arms are an inadequate
and inappropriate means of responding to security threats,
and that possession of them is immoral. Their production
diverts resources from integral human development, and
their employment not only has catastrophic humanitarian
and environmental consequences, but also threatens the
very existence of humanity.

Address to members of the diplomatic corps
accredited to the Holy See
Aula della Benedizione
January 10, 2022

A Culture of Death

The Culture of Indifference

In today's world, the sense of belonging to a single human family is fading, and the dream of working together for justice and peace seems an outdated utopia. What reigns instead is a cool, comfortable, and globalized indifference, born of deep disillusionment concealed behind a deceptive illusion: thinking that we are all-powerful, while failing to realize that we are all in the same boat. This illusion, unmindful of the great fraternal values, leads to a sort of cynicism. For that is the temptation we face if we go down the road of disenchantment and disappointment. . . . Isolation and withdrawal into one's own interests are never the way to restore hope and bring about renewal. Rather, it is closeness; it is the culture of encounter. Isolation, no; closeness, yes. Culture clash, no; culture of encounter, yes.

Fratelli tutti, 30

War Is Born in Human Hearts

A hundred years after the end of the First World War, as
we remember the young people killed in those battles and
the civilian populations torn apart, we are more conscious
than ever of the terrible lesson taught by fratricidal wars:
peace can never be reduced solely to a balance between
power and fear. To threaten others is to lower them to the
status of objects and to deny their dignity. This is why we
state once more that an escalation of intimidation, and the
uncontrolled proliferation of arms, is contrary to morality
and the search for true peace. Terror exerted over those
who are most vulnerable contributes to the exile of entire
populations who seek a place of peace. Political addresses
that tend to blame every evil on migrants and to deprive
the poor of hope are unacceptable. Rather, there is a need
to reaffirm that peace is based on respect for each person,
whatever his or her background, on respect for the law and
the common good, and on respect for the environment
entrusted to our care and for the richness of the moral tradition inherited from past generations.

Our thoughts turn in a particular way to all those children currently living in areas of conflict, and to all those
who work to protect their lives and defend their rights.
One out of every six children in our world are affected by
the violence of war or its effects, even when they are not
enrolled as child soldiers or held hostage by armed groups.
The witness given by those who work to defend them and
their dignity is most precious for the future of humanity.

In these days, we celebrate the seventieth anniversary of the Universal Declaration of Human Rights, adopted in the wake of the Second World War. In this context, let us also remember the observation of Pope John XXIII: "Man's awareness of his rights must inevitably lead him to the recognition of his duties. The possession of rights involves the duty of implementing those rights, for they are the expression of a man's personal dignity. And the possession of rights also involves their recognition and respect by others" [*Pacem in Terris*, 44].

Peace, in effect, is the fruit of a great political project grounded in the mutual responsibility and interdependence of human beings. But it is also a challenge that demands to be taken up ever anew. It entails a conversion of heart and soul; it is both interior and communal; and it has three inseparable aspects:

- Peace with oneself, rejecting inflexibility, anger, and impatience; in the words of Saint Francis de Sales, showing "a bit of sweetness towards oneself" in order to offer "a bit of sweetness to others."
- Peace with others: family members, friends, strangers, the poor and the suffering, being unafraid to encounter them and listen to what they have to say.
- Peace with all creation, rediscovering the grandeur of God's gift and our individual and shared responsibility as inhabitants of this world, citizens and builders of the future.

The politics of peace, conscious of and deeply concerned for every situation of human vulnerability, can always draw inspiration from the *Magnificat*, the hymn that Mary, the Mother of Christ the Savior and Queen of Peace, sang in the name of all mankind: "He has mercy on those who fear him in every generation. He has shown the strength of his arm; he has scattered the proud in their conceit. He has cast down the mighty from their thrones, and has lifted up the lowly; . . . for he has remembered his promise of mercy, the promise he made to our fathers, to Abraham and his children forever" (Lk 1:50–55).

> *Message for the LII World Day of Peace*
> *January 1, 2019*

War Eliminates All Development

"Deceit is in the mind of those who plan evil, but those who counsel peace have joy" (Prov 12:20). Yet there are those who seek solutions in war, frequently fueled by a breakdown in relations, hegemonic ambitions, abuses of power, fear of others, and a tendency to see diversity as an obstacle. War is not a ghost from the past but a constant threat. Our world is encountering growing difficulties on the slow path to peace upon which it had embarked and that had already begun to bear good fruit.

Since conditions that favor the outbreak of wars are once again increasing, I can only reiterate that war is the negation of all rights and a dramatic assault on the environment. If we want true integral human development for all, we must work tirelessly to avoid war between nations and peoples.

Fratelli tutti, 256–57

A Madness

I have prayed for those who fell in the Great War. The numbers are frightening: it is said that approximately eight million young soldiers fell and seven million civilians died. This tells us the extent to which war is madness! A madness from which humanity has not yet learned its lesson, because a second world war followed it and many more are still in progress today. But when will we learn from this lesson? I invite everyone to look to the Crucified Jesus to understand that hatred and evil are defeated through forgiveness and goodness, to understand that responding with war only increases evil and death!

Angelus
September 14, 2014

A Monster That Destroys Humanity and the World

War is always that monster that transforms itself with the change of epochs and continues to devour humanity. But the response to war is not another war; the response to weapons is not other weapons. And I ask myself: Who is selling weapons to the terrorists? Who sells weapons today to the

terrorists, who are carrying out massacres in other areas—
let us think of Africa, for example? It is a question that I
would like someone to answer. The response is not war, but
the response is fraternity. This is the challenge not only for
Iraq: it is the challenge for many regions in conflict and, ultimately, it is the challenge for the entire world: fraternity. Will
we be capable of creating fraternity among us, of building a
culture of brothers and sisters? Or will we continue with the
logic Cain began, war? Brotherhood, fraternity.

General Audience
Library of the Apostolic Palace
March 20, 2021

Conflicts Also Disfigure the Environment

It is foreseeable that, once certain resources have been
depleted, the scene will be set for new wars, albeit under the
guise of noble claims. War always does grave harm to the
environment and to the cultural riches of peoples, risks that
are magnified when one considers nuclear arms and biological weapons. "Despite the international agreements which
prohibit chemical, bacteriological and biological warfare, the
fact is that laboratory research continues to develop new
offensive weapons capable of altering the balance of nature"
[John Paul II, *Message for 1990 World Day Prayer*, 12]. Politics must pay greater attention to foreseeing new conflicts
and addressing the causes that can lead to them. But powerful financial interests prove most resistant to this effort,
and political planning tends to lack breadth of vision. What

would induce anyone, at this stage, to hold on to power only to be remembered for their inability to take action when it was urgent and necessary to do so?

Laudato si', 57

The "Piecemeal" World War

War, terrorist attacks, racial or religious persecution, and many other affronts to human dignity are judged differently, depending on how convenient it proves for certain, primarily economic, interests. What is true as long as it is convenient for someone in power stops being true once it becomes inconvenient. These situations of violence, sad to say, have become so common as to constitute a real "third world war" fought piecemeal.

Fratelli tutti, 25

Affecting the Little Ones

Brothers and sisters, never war! Never war! I think mostly of the children, of those who are deprived of the hope for a dignified life, of a future: dead children, wounded children, maimed children, orphaned children, children who have the remnants of war as toys, children who do not know how to smile. Stop, please! I ask you with all my heart. It is time to stop! Stop, please!

Angelus
July 27, 2014

We Listen to the Little Ones

Hope has the face of children. In the Middle East, for
years, an appalling number of young people have been
mourning violent deaths in their families and seeing
their native land threatened, often with their only pros-
pect being that of flight. This is the death of hope. All too
many children have spent most of their lives looking at
rubble instead of schools, hearing the deafening explosion
of bombs rather than the happy din of playgrounds. May
humanity listen—this is my plea—to the cry of children,
whose mouths proclaim the glory of God (cf. Ps 8:3). Only
by wiping away their tears will the world recover its dignity.

Address at the Conclusion of the Dialogue
Bari, Italy
July 7, 2018

Looking at Reality through the Eyes of Its Victims

Every war leaves our world worse than it was before. War
is a failure of politics and of humanity, a shameful capitulation, a stinging defeat before the forces of evil. Let us
not remain mired in theoretical discussions, but touch the
wounded flesh of the victims. Let us look once more at
all those civilians whose killing was considered "collateral
damage." Let us ask the victims themselves. Let us think of
the refugees and displaced, those who suffered the effects
of atomic radiation or chemical attacks, the mothers who

lost their children, and the boys and girls maimed or deprived of their childhood. Let us hear the true stories of these victims of violence, look at reality through their eyes, and listen with an open heart to the stories they tell. In this way, we will be able to grasp the abyss of evil at the heart of war. Nor will it trouble us to be deemed naive for choosing peace.

Fratelli tutti, 261

Terrorism Has Nothing to Do with True Religion

Sincere and humble worship of God "bears fruit not in discrimination, hatred and violence, but in respect for the sacredness of life, respect for the dignity and freedom of others, and loving commitment to the welfare of all" [Homily, Colombo, Sri Lanka, January 15, 2015]. Truly, "Whoever does not love does not know God, for God is love" (1 Jn 4:8). For this reason, terrorism is deplorable and threatens the security of people—be they in the East or the West, the North or the South—and disseminates panic, terror, and pessimism, but this is not due to religion, even when terrorists instrumentalize it. It is due, rather, to an accumulation of incorrect interpretations of religious texts and to policies linked to hunger, poverty, injustice, oppression, and pride. That is why it is so necessary to stop supporting terrorist movements fueled by financing, the provision of weapons and strategy, and by attempts to justify these movements, even using the media. All these must be regarded as international crimes that threaten security and world peace. Such terrorism must be condemned in all its forms and expressions. Religious convictions about the sacred meaning of human life permit us to recognize the fundamental values of our common humanity, values in the name of which we can and must cooperate, build and dialogue, pardon and grow; this will allow different voices to unite in creating a melody of sublime nobility and beauty, instead of fanatical cries of hatred.

At times, fundamentalist violence is unleashed in some groups, of whatever religion, by the rashness of their leaders. Yet, "The commandment of peace is inscribed in the depths of the religious traditions that we represent. . . . As religious leaders, we are called to be true 'people of dialogue,' to cooperate in building peace not as intermediaries but as authentic mediators. Intermediaries seek to give everyone a discount, ultimately in order to gain something for themselves. The mediator, on the other hand, is one who retains nothing for himself, but rather spends himself generously until he is consumed, knowing that the only gain is peace. Each one of us is called to be an artisan of peace, by uniting and not dividing, by extinguishing hatred and not holding on to it, by opening paths of dialogue and not by constructing new walls" [*Address to the International Meeting for Peace*, September 30, 2013].

Fratelli tutti, 283–84

The Criminal Folly of Nuclear Weapons

A Global Problem

Nuclear weapons are a global problem, affecting all nations, and impacting future generations and the planet that is our home. A global ethic is needed if we are to reduce the nuclear threat and work toward nuclear disarmament. Now more than ever, technological, social, and political interdependence urgently call for an ethic of solidarity, which encourages peoples to work together for a more secure world, and a future that is increasingly rooted in moral values and responsibility on a global scale.

The humanitarian consequences of nuclear weapons are predictable and planetary. While the focus is often placed on nuclear weapons' potential for mass killing, more attention must be given to the "unnecessary suffering" brought on by their use. Military codes and international law, among others, have long banned peoples from inflicting unnecessary suffering. If such suffering is banned in the waging of conventional war, then it should all the more be banned in nuclear conflict. There are those among us who are victims of these weapons; they warn us not to commit the same irreparable mistakes that have devastated populations and creation. I extend warm greetings to the *Hibakusha*, as well as other victims of nuclear weapons testing who are present at this meeting. I encourage them all to be prophetic voices, calling the human family to a deeper appreciation of beauty, love, cooperation, and fraternity, while reminding the world of the risks of nuclear weapons, which have the potential to destroy us and civilization.

Nuclear deterrence and the threat of mutually assured destruction cannot be the basis for an ethics of fraternity and peaceful coexistence among peoples and states. The youth of today and tomorrow deserve far more. They deserve a peaceful world order based on the unity of the human family, grounded on respect, cooperation, solidarity, and compassion. Now is the time to counter the logic of fear with the ethic of responsibility, and so foster a climate of trust and sincere dialogue.

Spending on nuclear weapons squanders the wealth of nations. To prioritize such spending is a mistake and a misallocation of resources that would be far better invested in the areas of integral human development, education, health, and the fight against extreme poverty. When these resources are squandered, the poor and the weak living on the margins of society pay the price.

The desire for peace, security, and stability is one of the deepest longings of the human heart. It is rooted in the Creator who makes all people members of the one human family. This desire can never be satisfied by military means alone, much less the possession of nuclear weapons and other weapons of mass destruction. Peace cannot "be reduced solely to maintaining a balance of power between enemies; nor is it brought about by dictatorship" (*Gaudium et Spes*, 78). Peace must be built on justice, socioeconomic development, freedom, respect for fundamental human rights, the participation of all in public affairs, and the building of trust between peoples. Pope Paul VI stated this succinctly in his encyclical *Populorum Progressio*: "Development is the new name for peace" (76). It is incumbent on us to adopt concrete actions that promote peace and security, while remaining always aware of the limitation of shortsighted approaches to problems of national and international security. We must be profoundly committed to strengthening mutual trust, for only through such trust can true and lasting peace among nations be established. . . .

I wish to encourage sincere and open dialogue between parties internal to each nuclear state, between various nuclear states, and between nuclear states and nonnuclear states. This dialogue must be inclusive, involving international organizations, religious communities, and civil society, and oriented toward the common good and not the protection of vested interests. "A world without nuclear weapons" is a goal shared by all nations and echoed by world leaders, as well as the aspiration of millions of men and women. The future and the survival of the human family hinge on moving beyond this ideal and ensuring that it becomes a reality.

I am convinced that the desire for peace and fraternity planted deep in the human heart will bear fruit in concrete ways to ensure that nuclear weapons are banned once and for all, to the benefit of our common home. The security of our own future depends on guaranteeing the peaceful security of others, for if peace, security, and stability are not established globally, they will not be enjoyed at all. Individually and collectively, we are responsible for the present and future well-being of our brothers and sisters. It is my great hope that this responsibility will inform our efforts in favor of nuclear disarmament, for a world without nuclear weapons is truly possible.

Message on the occasion of the Vienna Conference
on the Humanitarian Impact of Nuclear Weapons
December 7, 2014

A Tremendous Power

We must recognize that nuclear energy, biotechnology, information technology, knowledge of our DNA, and many other abilities that we have acquired have given us tremendous power. More precisely, they have given those with the knowledge, and especially the economic resources to use them, an impressive dominance over the whole of humanity and the entire world. Never has humanity had such power over itself, yet nothing ensures that it will be used wisely, particularly when we consider how it is currently being used. We need but think of the nuclear bombs dropped in the middle of the twentieth century, or the array of technology that Nazism, Communism, and other totalitarian regimes have employed to kill millions of people, to say nothing of the increasingly deadly arsenal of weapons available for modern warfare. In whose hands does all this power lie, or will it eventually end up? It is extremely risky for a small part of humanity to have it.

Laudato si', 104

A Great Deception

The Preamble and the first Article of the Charter of the United Nations set forth the foundations of the international juridical framework: peace, the pacific solution of disputes, and the development of friendly relations between the nations. Strongly opposed to such statements, and in practice denying them, is the constant tendency to the proliferation of arms, especially weapons of mass destruction, such as nuclear weapons. An ethics and a law based on the threat of mutual destruction—and possibly the destruction of all mankind—are self-contradictory and an affront to the entire framework of the United Nations, which would end up as "nations united by fear and distrust." There is urgent need to work for a world free of nuclear weapons, in full application of the Non-Proliferation Treaty, in letter and spirit, with the goal of a complete prohibition of these weapons.

The recent agreement reached on the nuclear question in a sensitive region of Asia and the Middle East is proof of the potential of political goodwill and of law, exercised with sincerity, patience, and constancy. I express my hope that this agreement will be lasting and efficacious, and bring forth the desired fruits with the cooperation of all the parties involved.

Address to the UN General Assembly
New York
September 25, 2015

Peace Cannot Be Built on Mutual Distrust

We must commit ourselves to a world without nuclear weapons, by fully implementing the Non-Proliferation Treaty, both in letter and spirit.

But why give ourselves this demanding and forward-looking goal in the present international context characterized by an unstable climate of conflict, which is both cause and indication of the difficulties encountered in advancing and strengthening the process of nuclear disarmament and nuclear nonproliferation?

If we take into consideration the principal threats to peace and security with their many dimensions in this multipolar world of the twenty-first century—as, for example, terrorism, asymmetrical conflicts, cybersecurity, environmental problems, and poverty—not a few doubts arise regarding the inadequacy of nuclear deterrence as an effective response to such challenges. These concerns are even greater when we consider the catastrophic humanitarian and environmental consequences that would follow from any use of nuclear weapons, with devastating, indiscriminate, and uncontainable effects, over time and space. Similar cause for concern arises when examining the waste of resources spent on nuclear issues for military purposes, which could instead be used for worthy priorities like the promotion of peace and integral human development, as well as the fight against poverty, and the implementation of the 2030 Agenda for Sustainable Development.

We need also to ask ourselves how sustainable is a stability based on fear, when it actually increases fear and undermines relationships of trust between peoples.

International peace and stability cannot be based on a false sense of security, on the threat of mutual destruction or total annihilation, or on simply maintaining a balance of power. Peace must be built on justice, on integral human development, on respect for fundamental human rights, on the protection of creation, on the participation of all in public life, on trust between peoples, on the support of peaceful institutions, on access to education and health, on dialogue and solidarity. From this perspective, we need to go beyond nuclear deterrence: the international community is called upon to adopt forward-looking strategies to promote the goal of peace and stability and to avoid short-sighted approaches to the problems surrounding national and international security.

In this context, the ultimate goal of the total elimination of nuclear weapons becomes both a challenge and a moral and humanitarian imperative. A concrete approach should promote a reflection on an ethics of peace and multilateral and cooperative security that goes beyond the fear and isolationism that prevail in many debates today. Achieving a world without nuclear weapons involves a long-term process, based on the awareness that "everything is connected" within the perspective of an integral ecology (see *Laudato si'*, 117, 138). The common destiny of humankind demands the pragmatic strengthening of dialogue and the building and consolidating of mechanisms of trust and cooperation, capable of creating the conditions for a world without nuclear weapons.

Growing interdependence and globalization mean that any response to the threat of nuclear weapons should be collective and concerted, based on mutual trust. This trust can be built only through dialogue that is truly directed to the common good and not to the protection of veiled or particular interests. Such dialogue, as far as possible, should include all: nuclear states, countries that do not possess nuclear weapons, the military and private sectors, religious communities, civil societies, and international organizations. And in this endeavor we must avoid those forms of mutual recrimination and polarization that hinder dialogue rather than encourage it. Humanity has the ability to work together in building up our common home; we have the freedom, intelligence, and capacity to lead and direct technology, to place limits on our power, and to put all this at the service of another type of progress: one that is more human, social, and integral.

This conference intends to negotiate a treaty inspired by ethical and moral arguments. It is an exercise in hope and it is my wish that it may also constitute a decisive step along the road toward a world without nuclear weapons. Although this is a significantly complex and long-term goal, it is not beyond our reach.

Message to the UN Conference to Negotiate
a Legally Binding Instrument to Prohibit
Nuclear Weapons, Leading towards
Their Total Elimination
New York
March 23, 2017

Atomic Weapons Are Senseless

A certain pessimism might make us think that "prospects for a world free from nuclear arms and for integral disarmament," the theme of your meeting, appear increasingly remote. Indeed, the escalation of the arms race continues unabated, and the price of modernizing and developing weaponry, not only nuclear weapons, represents a considerable expense for nations. As a result, the real priorities facing our human family, such as the fight against poverty; the promotion of peace; the undertaking of educational, ecological, and health-care projects; and the development of human rights, are relegated to second place.

Nor can we fail to be genuinely concerned by the catastrophic humanitarian and environmental effects of any employment of nuclear devices. If we also take into account the risk of an accidental detonation as a result of error of any kind, the threat of their use, as well as their very possession, is to be firmly condemned. For they exist in the service of a mentality of fear that affects not only the parties in conflict but the entire human race. International relations cannot be held captive to military force, mutual intimidation, and the parading of stockpiles of arms. Weapons of mass destruction, particularly nuclear weapons, create nothing but a false sense of security. They cannot constitute the basis for peaceful coexistence between members of the human family, which must rather be inspired by an ethics of solidarity. Essential in this regard is the witness given by the *Hibakusha*, the survivors of the bombing of Hiroshima and Nagasaki, together with other victims of nuclear arms testing. May their prophetic voice serve as a warning, above all for coming generations!

Furthermore, weapons that result in the destruction of the human race are senseless even from a tactical standpoint. For that matter, while true science is always at the service of humanity, in our time we are increasingly troubled by the misuse of certain projects originally conceived for a good cause. Suffice it to note that nuclear technologies are now spreading, also through digital communications, and that the instruments of international law have not prevented new states from joining those already in possession of nuclear weapons. The resulting scenarios are deeply disturbing if we consider the challenges of contemporary geopolitics, like terrorism or asymmetric warfare.

At the same time, a healthy realism continues to shine a light of hope on our unruly world. Recently, for example, in a historic vote at the United Nations, the majority of the members of the international community determined that nuclear weapons are not only immoral, but must also be considered an illegal means of warfare. This decision filled a significant juridical lacuna, inasmuch as chemical weapons, biological weapons, anti-personnel mines, and cluster bombs are all expressly prohibited by international conventions. Even more important is the fact that it was mainly the result of a "humanitarian initiative" sponsored by a significant alliance between civil society, states, international organizations, churches, academies, and groups of experts. . . .

It is therefore necessary, first of all, to reject the culture of waste and to care for individuals and peoples laboring under painful disparities through patient efforts to favor processes of solidarity over selfish and contingent interests. This also entails integrating the individual and the social dimensions through the application of the principle of subsidiarity, encouraging the contribution of all, as individuals and as groups. Lastly, there is a need to promote human beings in the indissoluble unity of soul and body, of contemplation and action.

In this way, progress that is both effective and inclusive can achieve the utopia of a world free of deadly instruments of aggression, contrary to the criticism of those who consider idealistic any process of dismantling arsenals. The teaching of John XXIII remains ever valid. In pointing to the goal of an integral disarmament, he stated, "Unless this process of disarmament be thoroughgoing and complete, and reach men's very souls, it is impossible to stop the arms race, or to reduce armaments, or—and this is the main thing—ultimately to abolish them entirely" (*Pacem in Terris*, 113).

The Church does not tire of offering the world this wisdom and the actions it inspires, conscious that integral development is the beneficial path that the human family is called to travel. I encourage you to carry forward this activity with patience and constancy, in the trust that the Lord is ever at our side. May he bless each of you and your efforts in the service of justice and peace. Thank you.

To Participants in the International Symposium
"Prospects for a World Free of Nuclear
Weapons and for Integral Disarmament"
Clementine Hall
November 10, 2017

Protect Every Life

From the Apostolic Journey to Japan
(November 23–26, 2019)

The Dream of a World Free of Nuclear Weapons

This place makes us deeply aware of the pain and horror that we human beings are capable of inflicting upon one another. The damaged cross and statue of Our Lady recently discovered in the Cathedral of Nagasaki remind us once more of the unspeakable horror suffered in the flesh by the victims of the bombing and their families.

One of the deepest longings of the human heart is for security, peace, and stability. The possession of nuclear and other weapons of mass destruction is not the answer to this desire; indeed they seem always to thwart it. Our world is marked by a perverse dichotomy that tries to defend and ensure stability and peace through a false sense of security sustained by a mentality of fear and mistrust, one that ends up poisoning relationships between peoples and obstructing any form of dialogue.

Peace and international stability are incompatible with attempts to build upon the fear of mutual destruction or the threat of total annihilation. They can be achieved only on the basis of a global ethic of solidarity and cooperation in the service of a future shaped by interdependence and shared responsibility in the whole human family of today and tomorrow.

Here in this city, which witnessed the catastrophic humanitarian and environmental consequences of a nuclear attack, our attempts to speak out against the arms race will never be enough. The arms race wastes precious resources that could be better used to benefit the integral development of peoples and to protect the natural environment. In a world where millions of children and families live in inhumane conditions, the money that is squandered and the fortunes made through the manufacture, upgrading, maintenance, and sale of ever more destructive weapons are an affront crying out to heaven.

A world of peace, free from nuclear weapons, is the aspiration of millions of men and women everywhere. To make this ideal a reality calls for involvement on the part of all: individuals, religious communities and civil society, countries that possess nuclear weapons and those that do not, the military and private sectors, and international organizations. Our response to the threat of nuclear weapons must be joint and concerted, inspired by the arduous yet constant effort to build mutual trust and thus surmount the current climate of distrust. In 1963, Saint John XXIII, writing in his encyclical letter *Pacem in Terris*, in addition to urging the prohibition of atomic weapons (see no. 112), stated that authentic and lasting international peace cannot rest on a balance of military power, but only upon mutual trust (see no. 113).

There is a need to break down the climate of distrust that risks leading to a dismantling of the international arms control framework. We are witnessing an erosion of multilateralism that is all the more serious in light of the growth of new forms of military technology. Such an approach seems highly incongruous in today's context of interconnectedness; it represents a situation that urgently calls for the attention and commitment of all leaders.

For her part, the Catholic Church is irrevocably committed to promoting peace between peoples and nations. This is a duty to which the Church feels bound before God and every man and woman in our world. We must never grow weary of working to support the principal international legal instruments of nuclear disarmament and nonproliferation, including the treaty on the prohibition of nuclear weapons. Last July, the bishops of Japan launched an appeal for the abolition of nuclear arms, and each August the Church in Japan holds a ten-day prayer meeting for peace. May prayer, tireless work in support of agreements, and insistence on dialogue be the most powerful "weapons" in which we put our trust and the inspiration of our efforts to build a world of justice and solidarity that can offer an authentic assurance of peace.

Convinced as I am that a world without nuclear weapons is possible and necessary, I ask political leaders not to forget that these weapons cannot protect us from current threats to national and international security. We need to ponder the catastrophic impact of their deployment, especially from a humanitarian and environmental standpoint, and reject heightening a climate of fear, mistrust, and hostility fomented by nuclear doctrines. The current state of our planet requires a serious reflection on how its resources can be employed in light of the complex and difficult implementation of the 2030 Agenda for Sustainable Development, in order to achieve the goal of an integrated human development. Saint Paul VI suggested as much in 1964, when he proposed the establishment of a Global Fund to assist those most impoverished peoples, drawn partially from military expenditures (*Populorum Progressio*, 51).

All of this necessarily calls for the creation of tools for ensuring trust and reciprocal development, and counts on leaders capable of rising to these occasions. It is a task that concerns and challenges every one of us. No one can be indifferent to the pain of millions of men and women whose sufferings trouble our consciences today. No one can turn a deaf ear to the plea of our brothers and sisters in need. No one can turn a blind eye to the ruin caused by a culture incapable of dialogue.

I ask you to join in praying each day for the conversion of hearts and for the triumph of a culture of life, reconciliation, and fraternity: a fraternity that can recognize and respect diversity in the quest for a common destiny.

I know that some here are not Catholics, but I am certain that we can all make our own the prayer for peace attributed to Saint Francis of Assisi:

> *Lord, make me an instrument of your peace:*
> *where there is hatred, let me sow love;*
> *where there is injury, pardon;*
> *where there is doubt, faith;*
> *where there is despair, hope;*
> *where there is darkness, light;*
> *where there is sadness, joy.*

In this striking place of remembrance that stirs us from our indifference, it is all the more meaningful that we turn to God with trust, asking him to teach us to be effective instruments of peace and to make every effort not to repeat the mistakes of the past.

May you and your families, and this entire nation, know the blessings of prosperity and social harmony!

> *Message on Nuclear Weapons*
> *Atomic Bomb Hypocenter Park (Nagasaki)*
> *November 24, 2019*

Nuclear Power for Military Purposes Is Immoral

> *For love of my brethren and friends, I say:*
> *"Peace upon you!" (Ps 122:8)*

God of mercy and Lord of history, to you we lift up our eyes from this place, where death and life have met, loss and rebirth, suffering and compassion.

Here, in an incandescent burst of lightning and fire, so many men and women, so many dreams and hopes, disappeared, leaving behind only shadows and silence.

In barely an instant, everything was devoured by a black hole of destruction and death. From that abyss of silence, we continue even today to hear the cries of those who are no longer. They came from different places, had different names, and some spoke different languages. Yet all were united in the same fate, in a terrifying hour that left its mark forever not only on the history of this country but on the face of humanity.

Here I pay homage to all the victims, and I bow before the strength and dignity of those who, having survived those first moments, for years afterward bore in the flesh immense suffering, and in their spirit seeds of death that drained their vital energy.

I felt a duty to come here as a pilgrim of peace, to stand in silent prayer, to recall the innocent victims of such violence, and to bear in my heart the prayers and yearnings of the men and women of our time, especially the young, who long for peace, who work for peace, and who sacrifice themselves for peace. I have come to this place of memory and of hope for the future, bringing with me the cry of the poor, who are always the most helpless victims of hatred and conflict.

It is my humble desire to be the voice of the voiceless, who witness with concern and anguish the growing tensions of our own time: the unacceptable inequalities and injustices that threaten human coexistence, the grave inability to care for our common home, and the constant outbreak of armed conflict, as if these could guarantee a future of peace.

With deep conviction I wish once more to declare that the use of atomic energy for purposes of war is today, more than ever, a crime not only against the dignity of human beings but against any possible future for our common home. The use of atomic energy for purposes of war is immoral, just as the possessing of nuclear weapons is immoral, as I already said two years ago. We will be judged on this. Future generations will rise to condemn our failure if we spoke of peace but did not act to bring it about among the peoples of the earth. How can we speak of peace even as we build terrifying new weapons of war? How can we speak about peace even as we justify illegitimate actions by speeches filled with discrimination and hate?

I am convinced that peace is no more than an empty word unless it is founded on truth, built up in justice, animated and perfected by charity, and attained in freedom.

Building peace in truth and justice entails acknowledging that "people frequently differ widely in knowledge, virtue, intelligence, and wealth" (*Pacem in Terris*, 87), and that this can never justify the attempt to impose our own particular interests upon others. Indeed, those differences call for even greater responsibility and respect. Political communities may legitimately differ from one another in terms of culture or economic development, but all are called to commit themselves to work "for the common cause," for the good of all (88).

Indeed, if we really want to build a more just and secure society, we must let the weapons fall from our

hands. "No one can love with offensive weapons in their
hands" (Saint Paul VI, *United Nations address*, October 4,
1965). When we yield to the logic of arms and distance
ourselves from the practice of dialogue, we forget to our
detriment that, even before causing victims and ruination,
weapons can create nightmares; "they call for enormous
expenses, interrupt projects of solidarity and of useful
labor, and warp the outlook of nations." How can we propose peace if we constantly invoke the threat of nuclear
war as a legitimate recourse for the resolution of conflicts?
May the abyss of pain endured here remind us of bound-
aries that must never be crossed. A true peace can only be
an unarmed peace. For "peace is not merely the absence of
war . . . but must be built up ceaselessly" (*Gaudium et Spes*,
78). It is the fruit of justice, development, solidarity, care
for our common home, and the promotion of the common
good, as we have learned from the lessons of history.

To remember, to journey together, to protect. These
three moral imperatives here in Hiroshima assume even
more powerful and universal significance, and can open a
path to peace. For this reason, we cannot allow present and
future generations to lose the memory of what happened
here. It is a memory that ensures and encourages the
building of a more fair and fraternal future; an expansive
memory, capable of awakening the consciences of all men
and women, especially those who today play a crucial role
in the destiny of the nations; a living memory that helps us
say in every generation: never again!

That is why we are called to journey together with a
gaze of understanding and forgiveness, to open the horizon

to hope and to bring a ray of light amid the many clouds that today darken the sky. Let us open our hearts to hope, and become instruments of reconciliation and peace. This will always be possible if we are able to protect one another and realize that we are joined by a common destiny. Our world, interconnected not only by globalization but by the very earth we have always shared, demands, today more than ever, that interests exclusive to certain groups or sectors be left to one side, in order to achieve the greatness of those who struggle co-responsibly to ensure a common future.

In a single plea to God and to all men and women of goodwill, on behalf of all the victims of atomic bombings and experiments, and of all conflicts, let us together cry out from our hearts: Never again war, never again the clash of arms, never again so much suffering! May peace come in our time and to our world. O God, you have promised us that "mercy and faithfulness have met, justice and peace have embraced; faithfulness shall spring from the earth, and justice look down from heaven" (Ps 84:11–12).

Come, Lord, for it is late, and where destruction has abounded, may hope also abound today that we can write and achieve a different future. Come, Lord, Prince of Peace! Make us instruments and reflections of your peace!

"For love of my brethren and friends, I say: 'Peace upon you!'" (Ps 122:8).

Meeting for Peace
Peace Memorial (Hiroshima)
November 24, 2019

Hiroshima Is a Catechesis on Cruelty

Hiroshima was a true human catechesis on cruelty. Cruelty . . . and there I reaffirmed that the use of nuclear weapons is immoral—this must also be included in the *Catechism of the Catholic Church*—and not only its use, but also its possession because an accident [due to] possession, or the madness of some government leader, a person's madness can destroy humanity. Let us think about that quote from Einstein: "World War IV will be fought with sticks and stones."

I return to the possession of nuclear industries. An accident can always occur. You have experienced this, as well as the triple disaster [of Fukashima] that destroyed so much. Nuclear power is at its limits. Let us exclude weapons because they are destructive. But the use of nuclear power is very much at its limits because we have not reached complete safety yet. We have not reached it. You could say to me, "Yes, you could have a disaster due to lack of safety with electricity too." But it is a small disaster. A nuclear disaster, from a nuclear plant, will be a huge disaster. And safety measures have not yet been developed. I—but it is my personal opinion—would not use nuclear energy until its use is completely safe. But I am profane in this and I am expressing an idea. Some say nuclear energy goes against the care of creation, that it will destroy it and that it must stop. It is under discussion. I stop at safety. It does not have the safety measures to avoid a disaster. Yes, there is one in the world every ten years, but then it [affects] creation: the disaster of a nuclear power on creation and also on people.

Press conference on return flight from Japan
November 26, 2019

The Only Solution to Conflicts Is Dialogue

In the footsteps of my predecessors, I have also come to implore God and to invite all persons of goodwill to encourage and promote every necessary means of dissuasion so that the destruction generated by atomic bombs in Hiroshima and Nagasaki will never take place again in human history. History teaches us that conflicts and misunderstandings between peoples and nations can find valid solutions only through dialogue, the only weapon worthy of humanity and capable of ensuring lasting peace. I am convinced of the need to deal with the nuclear question on the multilateral plane, promoting a political and institutional process capable of creating a broader international consensus and action.

A culture of encounter and dialogue, marked by wisdom, insight, and breadth of vision, is essential for building a more just and fraternal world. Japan has recognized the importance of promoting personal contacts in the fields of education, culture, sport, and tourism, knowing that these can contribute in no small measure to the harmony, justice, solidarity, and reconciliation that are the mortar of the edifice of peace.

Meeting with the authorities and diplomatic corps
Kantei, Great Hall (Tokyo)
November 25, 2019

Peace and Fraternity

From the Apostolic Journey to Iraq
(March 5–8, 2021)

Fraternity Is Nourished by Solidarity

Fraternal coexistence calls for patient and honest dialogue, protected by justice and respect for law. This task is not easy; it demands hard work and a commitment on the part of all to set aside rivalries and contrapositions and instead to speak with one another from our deepest identity as fellow children of the one God and Creator. On the basis of this principle, the Holy See, in Iraq as elsewhere, tirelessly appeals to competent authorities to grant all religious communities recognition, respect, rights, and protection. I appreciate the efforts already being made in this regard, and I join men and women of goodwill in calling for these efforts to continue for the benefit of the nation.

A society that bears the imprint of fraternal unity is one whose members live in solidarity with one another. "Solidarity helps us to regard others . . . as our neighbors, companions on our journey" (*Message for the 2021 World*

Day of Peace). It is a virtue that leads us to carry out concrete acts of care and service with particular concern for the vulnerable and those most in need. Here, I think of all those who have lost family members and loved ones, home and livelihood due to violence, persecution, or terrorism. I think too of those who continue to struggle for security and the means of personal and economic survival at a time of growing unemployment and poverty. The "consciousness that we are responsible for the fragility of others" (*Fratelli tutti*, 115) ought to inspire every effort to create concrete opportunities for progress, not only economically, but also in terms of education and care for our common home. Following a crisis, it is not enough simply to rebuild; we need to rebuild well, so that all can enjoy a dignified life. We never emerge from a crisis the same as we were; we emerge from it either better or worse.

As governmental leaders and diplomats, you are called to foster this spirit of fraternal solidarity. It is necessary, but not sufficient, to combat the scourge of corruption, misuse of power, and disregard for law. Also necessary is the promotion of justice and the fostering of honesty, transparency, and the strengthening of the institutions responsible in this regard. In this way, stability within society grows and a healthy politics arises, able to offer to all, especially the young of whom there are so many in this country, sure hope for a better future. . . .

I come as a penitent, asking forgiveness of heaven and my brothers and sisters for so much destruction and cruelty. I come as a pilgrim of peace in the name of Christ, the Prince of Peace. How much we have prayed in these years for peace in Iraq! Saint John Paul II spared no initiatives and above all offered his prayers and sufferings for this intention. And God listens, he always listens! It is up to us to listen to him and to walk in his ways. May the clash of arms be silenced! May their spread be curbed, here and everywhere! May partisan interests cease, those outside interests uninterested in the local population. May the voice of builders and peacemakers find a hearing! The voice of the humble, the poor, the ordinary men and women who want to live, work, and pray in peace. May there be an end to acts of violence and extremism, factions and intolerance! May room be made for all those citizens who seek to cooperate in building up this country through dialogue and through frank, sincere, and constructive discussion—citizens committed to reconciliation and prepared, for the common good, to set aside their own interests. Iraq has sought in these years to lay the foundations for a democratic society. For this, it is essential to ensure the participation of all political, social, and religious groups and to guarantee the fundamental rights of all citizens. May no one be considered a second-class citizen. I encourage the strides made so far on this journey and I trust that they will strengthen tranquility and concord.

The international community also has a role to play in the promotion of peace in this land and in the Middle East as a whole. As we have seen during the lengthy conflict in neighboring Syria—which began ten years ago these very days!—the challenges facing our world today engage the entire human family. They call for cooperation on a global scale in order to address, among other things, the economic inequalities and regional tensions that threaten the stability of these lands. I thank the countries and international organizations working in Iraq to rebuild and to provide humanitarian assistance to refugees, the internally displaced, and those attempting to return home, by making food, water, shelter, health care, and hygiene services available throughout the country, together with programs of reconciliation and peacebuilding. Here I cannot fail to mention the many agencies, including a number of Catholic agencies, that for many years have been committed to helping the people of this country. Meeting the basic needs of so many of our brothers and sisters is an act of charity and justice, and contributes to a lasting peace. It is my prayerful hope that the international community will not withdraw from the Iraqi people the outstretched hand of friendship and constructive engagement, but will continue to act in a spirit of shared responsibility with the local authorities, without imposing political or ideological interests.

Religion, by its very nature, must be at the service of peace and fraternity. The name of God cannot be used to justify acts of murder, exile, terrorism, and oppression. On the contrary, God, who created human beings equal in dignity and rights, calls us to spread the values of love, goodwill, and concord. In Iraq, too, the Catholic Church desires to be a friend to all and, through interreligious dialogue, to cooperate constructively with other religions in serving the cause of peace. The age-old presence of Christians in this land, and their contributions to the life of the nation, constitute a rich heritage that they wish to continue to place at the service of all. Their participation in public life, as citizens with full rights, freedoms, and responsibilities, will testify that a healthy pluralism of religious beliefs, ethnicities, and cultures can contribute to the nation's prosperity and harmony.

Meeting with authorities, civil society,
and the diplomatic corps
Baghdad
March 5, 2021

Weaving a Single Fraternity

The love of Christ summons us to set aside every kind of self-centeredness or competition; it impels us to universal communion and challenges us to form a community of brothers and sisters who accept and care for one another. Here I think of the familiar image of a carpet. The different churches present in Iraq, each with its age-old historical, liturgical, and spiritual patrimony, are like so many individual colored threads that, woven together, make up a single beautiful carpet, one that displays not only our fraternity but points also to its source. For God himself is the artist who imagined this carpet, patiently wove it, and carefully mends it, desiring us ever to remain closely knit as his sons and daughters. May we thus take to heart the admonition of Saint Ignatius of Antioch: "Let nothing exist among you that may divide you . . . but let there be one prayer, one mind, one hope, in love and in joy." How important is this witness of fraternal union in a world all too often fragmented and torn by division! Every effort made to build bridges between ecclesial, parish, and diocesan communities and institutions will serve as a prophetic gesture on the part of the Church in Iraq and a fruitful response to Jesus's prayer that all may be one (see Jn 17:21).

Pastors and faithful, priests, religious, and catechists share, albeit in distinct ways, in the responsibility for advancing the Church's mission. At times, misunderstandings can arise and we can experience certain tensions; these are the knots that hinder the weaving of fraternity. They are knots we carry within ourselves; after all, we are all sinners. Yet these knots can be untied by grace, by a greater love; they can be loosened by the medicine of forgiveness and by fraternal dialogue, by patiently bearing one another's burdens (see Gal 6:2) and strengthening each other in moments of trial and difficulty....

I am thinking especially of the young. Young people everywhere are a sign of promise and hope, but particularly in this country. Here you have not only priceless archaeological treasures but also inestimable treasure for the future: the young! Young people are your treasure; they need you to care for them, to nurture their dreams, to accompany their growth and to foster their hope. Even though they are young, their patience has already been sorely tried by the conflicts of these years. Yet let us never forget that, together with the elderly, they are the point of the diamond in this country, the richest fruit of the tree. It is up to us to cultivate their growth in goodness and to nurture them with hope.

Meeting with bishops, priests, religious,
seminarians, and catechists
Baghdad
March 5, 2021

We Look to Heaven and Journey on Earth

This blessed place brings us back to our origins, to the sources of God's work, to the birth of our religions. Here, where Abraham our father lived, we seem to have returned home. It was here that Abraham heard God's call; it was from here that he set out on a journey that would change history. We are the fruits of that call and that journey. God asked Abraham to raise his eyes to heaven and to count its stars (see Gen 15:5). In those stars, he saw the promise of his descendants; he saw us. Today we—Jews, Christians, and Muslims—together with our brothers and sisters of other religions honor our father Abraham by doing as he did: *we look up to heaven and we journey on earth.*

We look up to heaven. Thousands of years later, as we look up to the same sky, those same stars appear. They illumine the darkest nights because they shine *together.* Heaven thus imparts a message of unity: the Almighty above invites us never to separate ourselves from our neighbors. The *otherness* of God points us toward *others,* toward our brothers and sisters. Yet if we want to preserve fraternity, we must not lose sight of heaven. May we—the descendants of Abraham and the representatives of different religions—sense that, above all, we have this role: to help our brothers and sisters to raise their eyes and prayers to heaven. We all need this because we are not self-sufficient. Man is not omnipotent; we cannot make it on our own. If we exclude God, we end up worshiping the things of this earth. Worldly goods, which lead so many people to be unconcerned with God and others, are not the reason why we journey on earth. We raise our eyes to heaven in order to raise ourselves from the depths of our vanity; we serve God in order to be set free from enslavement to our egos, because God urges us to love. This is true religiosity: to worship God and to love our neighbor. In today's world, which often forgets or presents distorted images of the Most High, believers are called to bear witness to his goodness, to show his paternity through our fraternity.

From this place, where faith was born, from the land of our father Abraham, let us affirm that *God is merciful* and that the greatest blasphemy is to profane his name by hating our brothers and sisters. Hostility, extremism, and violence are not born of a religious heart: they are betrayals of religion. We believers cannot be silent when terrorism abuses religion; indeed, we are called unambiguously to dispel all misunderstandings. Let us not allow the light of heaven to be overshadowed by the clouds of hatred! Dark clouds of terrorism, war, and violence have gathered over this country. All its ethnic and religious communities have suffered. In particular, I would like to mention the Yazidi community, which has mourned the deaths of many men and witnessed thousands of women, girls, and children kidnapped, sold as slaves, and subjected to physical violence and forced conversions. Today, let us pray for those who have endured these sufferings, for those who are still dispersed and abducted, that they may soon return home. And let us pray that freedom of conscience and freedom of religion will everywhere be recognized and respected; these are fundamental rights because they make us free to contemplate the heaven for which we were created.

When terrorism invaded the north of this beloved country, it wantonly destroyed part of its magnificent religious heritage, including the churches, monasteries, and places of worship of various communities. Yet, even at that dark time, some stars kept shining. I think of the young Muslim volunteers of Mosul, who helped to repair churches and monasteries, building fraternal friendships on the rubble of hatred, and those Christians and Muslims who today are restoring mosques and churches together. Professor Ali Thajeel spoke too of the return of pilgrims to this city. Making pilgrimages to holy places is important, for it is the most beautiful sign on earth of our yearning for heaven. To love and protect holy places, therefore, is an existential necessity, in memory of our father Abraham, who in various places raised to heaven altars of the Lord (see Gen 12:7–8; 13:18; 22:9). May the great Patriarch help us to make our respective sacred places oases of peace and encounter for all! By his fidelity to God, Abraham became a blessing for all peoples (see Gen 12:3); may our presence here today, in his footsteps, be a sign of blessing and hope for Iraq, for the Middle East and for the whole world. Heaven has not grown weary of the earth: God loves every people, every one of his daughters and sons! Let us never tire of *looking up to heaven*, of looking up to those same stars that, in his day, our father Abraham contemplated.

We journey on earth. For Abraham, looking up to heaven, rather than being a distraction, was an incentive to journey on earth, to set out on a path that, through his descendants, would lead to every time and place. It all started from here, with the Lord who brought him forth from Ur (see Gen 15:7). His was a *journey outward*, one that involved sacrifices. Abraham had to leave his land, home, and family. Yet by giving up his own family, he became the father of a family of peoples. Something similar also happens to us: on our own journey, we are called to leave behind those ties and attachments that, by keeping us enclosed in our own groups, prevent us from welcoming God's boundless love and from seeing others as our brothers and sisters. We need to move beyond ourselves, because *we need one another*. The pandemic has made us realize that "no one is saved alone" (*Fratelli tutti*, 54). Still, the temptation to withdraw from others is never-ending, yet at the same time we know that "the notion of 'every man for himself' will rapidly degenerate into a free-for-all that would prove worse than any pandemic" (36). Amid the tempests we are currently experiencing, such isolation will not save us. Nor will an arms race or the erection of walls that will only make us all the more distant and aggressive. Nor the idolatry of money, for it closes us in on ourselves and creates chasms of inequality that engulf humanity. Nor can we be saved by consumerism, which numbs the mind and deadens the heart.

The way that heaven points out for our journey is another: *the way of peace*. It demands, especially amid the tempest, that we row together on the same side. It is shameful that, while all of us have suffered from the crisis of the pandemic, especially here, where conflicts have caused so much suffering, anyone should be concerned simply for his own affairs. There will be no peace without sharing and acceptance, without a justice that ensures equity and advancement for all, beginning with those most vulnerable. There will be no peace unless peoples extend a hand to other peoples. There will be no peace as long as we see others as *them* and not *us*. There will be no peace as long as our alliances are *against* others, for alliances of some against others only increase divisions. Peace does not demand winners or losers, but rather brothers and sisters who, for all the misunderstandings and hurts of the past, are journeying from conflict to unity. Let us ask for this in praying for the whole Middle East. Here I think especially of neighboring war-torn Syria.

The Patriarch Abraham, who today brings us together in unity, was a prophet of the Most High. An ancient prophecy says that the peoples "shall beat their swords into plowshares, and their spears into pruning hooks" (Is 2:4). This prophecy has not been fulfilled; on the contrary, swords and spears have turned into missiles and bombs. From where, then, can the journey of peace begin? From the decision not to have enemies. Anyone with the courage to look at the stars, anyone who believes in God, has no enemies to fight. He or she has only one enemy to face, an enemy that stands at the door of the heart and knocks to enter. That enemy is *hatred*. While some try to have enemies more than to be friends, while many seek their own profit at the expense of others, those who look at the stars of the promise, those who follow the ways of God, cannot be *against* someone, but *for* everyone. They cannot justify any form of imposition, oppression, and abuse of power; they cannot adopt an attitude of belligerence.

Dear friends, is all this possible? Father Abraham, who was able to hope against all hope (see Rom 4:18), encourages us. Throughout history, we have frequently pursued goals that are overly worldly and journeyed on our own, but with the help of God, we can change for the better. It is up to us, today's humanity, especially those of us, believers of all religions, to turn instruments of hatred into instruments of peace. It is up to us to appeal firmly to the leaders of nations to make the increasing proliferation of arms give way to the distribution of food for all. It is up to us to silence mutual accusations in order to make heard the cry of the oppressed and discarded in our world: all too many people lack food, medicine, education, rights, and dignity! It is up to us to shed light on the shady maneuvers that revolve around money and to demand that money not end up always and only reinforcing the unbridled luxury of a few. It is up to us to preserve our common home from our predatory aims. It is up to us to remind the world that human life has value for what it is and not for what it has. That the lives of the unborn, the elderly, migrants, and men and women, whatever the color of their skin or their nationality, are always sacred and count as much as the lives of everyone else! It is up to us to have the courage to *lift up our eyes and look at the stars*, the stars that our father Abraham saw, the stars of the promise.

The journey of Abraham was a blessing of peace. Yet it was not easy: he had to face struggles and unforeseen events. We too have a rough journey ahead, but like the great Patriarch, we need to take *concrete steps* to set out and seek the face of others, to share memories, gazes and silences, stories and experiences. I was struck by the testimony of Dawood and Hasan, a Christian and a Muslim, respectively, who, undaunted by the differences between them, studied and worked together. Together they built the future and realized that they are brothers. In order to move forward, we too need to achieve something good and concrete together. This is the way, especially for young people, who must not see their dreams cut short by the conflicts of the past! It is urgent to teach them fraternity, to teach them to look at the stars. This is a real emergency; it will be the most effective vaccine for a future of peace. For you, dear young people, are our present and our future!

Only with others can the wounds of the past be healed. Rafah told us of the heroic example of Najy, from the Sabean Mandean community, who lost his life in an attempt to save the family of his Muslim neighbor. How many people here, amid the silence and indifference of the world, have embarked upon journeys of fraternity! Rafah also told us of the unspeakable sufferings of the war that forced many to abandon home and country in search of a future for their children. Thank you, Rafah, for having shared with us your firm determination to stay here, in the land of your fathers. May those who were unable to do so, and had to flee, find a kindly welcome, befitting those who are vulnerable and suffering.

It was precisely through hospitality, a distinctive feature of these lands, that Abraham was visited by God and given the gift of a son, when it seemed that all hope was past (see Gen 18:1–10). Brothers and sisters of different religions, here we find ourselves at home, and from here, together, we wish to commit ourselves to fulfilling God's dream that the human family may become hospitable and welcoming to all his children; that looking up to the same heaven, it will journey in peace on the same earth.

Interfaith meeting
Ur Plain
March 6, 2021

Love Wins

Jesus, who is Wisdom in person, completes this reversal in the Gospel, and he does so with his very first sermon, with the Beatitudes. The reversal is total: the poor, those who mourn, the persecuted are all called blessed. How is this possible? For the world, it is the rich, the powerful, and the famous who are blessed! It is those with wealth and means who count! But not for God: It is no longer the rich who are great, but the poor in spirit; not those who can impose their will on others, but those who are gentle with all. Not those acclaimed by the crowds, but those who show mercy to their brothers and sisters. At this point, we may wonder: If I live as Jesus asks, What do I gain? Don't I risk letting others lord it over me? Is Jesus's invitation worthwhile or a lost cause? That invitation is not worthless, but wise.

Jesus's invitation is wise because love, which is the heart of the Beatitudes, even if it seems weak in the world's eyes, in fact always triumphs. On the cross, it proved stronger than sin; in the tomb, it vanquished death. That same love made the martyrs victorious in their trials—and how many martyrs have there been in the last century, more even than in the past! Love is our strength, the source of strength for those of our brothers and sisters who here too have suffered prejudice and indignities, mistreatment and persecutions for the name of Jesus. Yet while the power, the glory, and the vanity of the world pass away, love remains. As the Apostle Paul told us, "Love never ends" (1 Cor 13:8). To live a life shaped by the Beatitudes, then, is to make passing things eternal, to bring heaven to earth.

But how do we practice the Beatitudes? They do not ask us to do extraordinary things, feats beyond our abilities. They ask for daily *witness*. The blessed are those who live meekly, who show mercy wherever they happen to be, who are pure of heart wherever they live. To be blessed, we do not need to become occasional heroes, but *to become witnesses* day after day. Witness is the way to embody the wisdom of Jesus. That is how the world is changed: not by power and might, but by the Beatitudes. For that is what Jesus did: he lived to the end what he said from the beginning. Everything depends on bearing witness to the love of Jesus, that same charity that Saint Paul magnificently describes in today's second reading [1 Cor 13:4–7]. Let us see how he presents it.

First, Paul says that "love is patient" (v. 4). We were not expecting this adjective. Love seems synonymous with goodness, generosity, and good works, yet Paul says that charity is above all *patient*. The Bible speaks first and foremost of God's patience. Throughout history, men and women proved constantly unfaithful to the covenant with God, falling into the same old sins. Yet instead of growing weary and walking away, the Lord always remained faithful, forgave and began anew. This patience to begin anew each time is the first quality of love, because love is not irritable, but always starts over again. Love does not grow weary and despondent, but always presses ahead. It does not get discouraged, but stays creative. Faced with evil, it does not give up or surrender. Those who love do not close in on themselves when things go wrong, but respond to evil with good, mindful of the triumphant wisdom of the cross. God's witnesses are like that: not passive or fatalistic, at the mercy of happenings, feelings, or immediate events. Instead, they are constantly hopeful, because they are grounded in the love that "bears all things, believes all things, hopes all things, endures all things" (v. 7).

We can ask ourselves: how do we react to situations that are not right? In the face of adversity, there are always two temptations. The first is flight: we can run away, turn our backs, trying to keep aloof from it all. The second is to react with anger, with a show of force. Such was the case of the disciples in Gethsemane: in their bewilderment, many fled and Peter took up the sword. Yet neither flight nor the sword achieved anything. Jesus, on the other hand, changed history. How? With the humble power of love, with his patient witness. This is what we are called to do, and this is how God fulfills his promises.

Promises. The wisdom of Jesus, embodied in the Beatitudes, calls for witness and offers the reward contained in the divine promises. For each Beatitude is immediately followed by a promise: those who practice them will possess the kingdom of heaven, they will be comforted, they will be satisfied, they will see God . . . (see Mt 5:3–12). God's promises guarantee unrivaled joy and never disappoint. But how are they fulfilled? *Through our weaknesses.* God makes blessed those who travel the path of their inner poverty to the very end.

This is the way; there is no other. Let us look to the Patriarch Abraham. God promised him a great offspring, but he and Sarah are now elderly and childless. Yet it is precisely in their patient and faithful old age that God works wonders and gives them a son. Let us also look to Moses: God promises that he will free the people from slavery, and to do so he asks Moses to speak to Pharaoh. Even though Moses says he is not good with words, it is through his words that God will fulfill his promise. Let us look to Our Lady, who under the Law could not have a child, yet was called to become a mother. And let us look to Peter: he denies the Lord, yet he is the very one whom Jesus calls to strengthen his brethren. Dear brothers and sisters, at times we may feel helpless and useless. We should never give in to this, because God wants to work wonders precisely through our weaknesses.

God loves to do that, and tonight, eight times, he has spoken to us the word *ṭūb'ā* [blessed], in order to make us realize that, with him, we truly are "blessed." Of course, we experience trials, and we frequently fall, but let us not forget that, with Jesus, we are blessed. Whatever the world takes from us is nothing compared to the tender and patient love with which the Lord fulfills his promises. Dear sister, dear brother, perhaps when you look at your hands they seem empty, perhaps you feel disheartened and unsatisfied by life. If so, do not be afraid: the Beatitudes are for you. For you who are afflicted, who hunger and thirst for justice, who are persecuted. The Lord promises you that your name is written on his heart, written in heaven!

Today I thank God with you and for you, because here, where *wisdom* arose in ancient times, so many *witnesses* have arisen in our own time, often overlooked by the news, yet precious in God's eyes. Witnesses who, by living the Beatitudes, are helping God to fulfill his *promises* of peace.

Homily
Baghdad
March 6, 2021

Jesus at Our Side

Our gathering here today shows that terrorism and death never have the last word. The last word belongs to God and to his Son, the conqueror of sin and death. Even amid the ravages of terrorism and war, we can see, with the eyes of faith, the triumph of life over death. You have before you the example of your fathers and mothers in faith, who worshiped and praised God in this place. They persevered with unwavering hope along their earthly journey, trusting in God who never disappoints and who constantly sustains us by his grace. The great spiritual legacy they left behind continues to live in you. Embrace this legacy! It is your strength! Now is the time to rebuild and to start afresh, relying on the grace of God, who guides the destinies of all individuals and peoples. You are not alone! The entire Church is close to you, with prayers and concrete charity. And in this region, so many people opened their doors to you in time of need.

Dear friends, this is the time to restore not just buildings but also the bonds of community that unite communities and families, the young and the old together. The prophet Joel says, "Your sons and your daughters shall prophecy, your old men shall dream dreams, and your young men shall see visions" (3:1). When the old and the young come together, what happens? The old dream dreams, they dream of a future for the young. And the young can take those dreams and prophecy, make them reality. When old and young come together, we preserve and pass on the gifts that God gives. We look upon our children, knowing that they will inherit not only a land, a culture, and a tradition, but also the living fruits of faith that are God's blessings upon this land. So I encourage you: Do not forget who you are and where you come from! Do not forget the bonds that hold you together! Do not forget to preserve your roots!

Surely, there will be moments when faith can waver, when it seems that God does not see or act. This was true for you in the darkest days of the war, and it is true too in these days of global health crisis and great insecurity. At times like these, remember that Jesus is by your side. Do not stop dreaming! Do not give up! Do not lose hope! From heaven the saints are watching over us. Let us pray to them and never tire of begging their intercession. There are also the saints next door, "who, living in our midst, reflect God's presence" (*Gaudate et Exsultate*, 7). This land has many of them, because it is a land of many holy men and women. Let them accompany you to a better future, a future of hope. . . .

At all times, let us offer thanks to God for his gracious gifts and ask him to grant his peace, forgiveness, and fraternity to this land and its people. Let us pray tirelessly for the conversion of hearts and for the triumph of a culture of life, reconciliation, and fraternal love between all men and women, with respect for differences and diverse religious traditions, in the effort to build a future of unity and cooperation between all people of goodwill—a fraternal love that recognizes "the fundamental values of our common humanity, values in the name of which we can and must cooperate, build and dialogue, pardon and grow" (*Fratelli tutti*, 283).

As I arrived on the helicopter, I saw the statue of Mary on this Church of the Immaculate Conception. To her I entrusted the rebirth of this city. Our Lady does not only protect us from on high but comes down to us with a Mother's love. Her image here has met with mistreatment and disrespect, yet the face of the Mother of God continues to look upon us with love. For that is what mothers do: they console, they comfort, and they give life. I would like to say a heartfelt thank-you to all the mothers and women of this country, women of courage who continue to give life, in spite of wrongs and hurts. May women be respected and protected! May they be shown respect and provided with opportunities!

Address to the community of Qaraqosh
March 7, 2021

Church and Society Open to All

In the Gospel (Jn 2:13–25), we see how Jesus drove out from the Temple in Jerusalem the moneychangers and all the buyers and sellers. Why did Jesus do something this forceful and provocative? He did it because the Father sent him to cleanse the temple—not only the Temple of stone, but above all the temple of our heart. Jesus could not tolerate his Father's house becoming a marketplace (see Jn 2:16); neither does he want our hearts to be places of turmoil, disorder, and confusion. Our heart must be cleansed, put in order, and purified. Of what? Of the falsehoods that stain it, from hypocritical duplicity. All of us have these. They are diseases that harm the heart, soil our lives, and make them insincere. We need to be cleansed of the deceptive securities that would barter our faith in God with passing things, with temporary advantages. We need the baneful temptations of power and money to be swept from our hearts and from the Church. To cleanse our hearts, we need to dirty our hands, to feel accountable, and not to simply look on as our brothers and sisters are suffering. How do we purify our hearts? By our own efforts, we cannot; we need Jesus. He has the power to conquer our evils, to heal our diseases, to rebuild the temple of our heart.

To show this, and as a sign of his authority, Jesus goes on to say, "Destroy this temple, and in three days I will raise it up" (Jn 2:19). Jesus Christ, he alone, can cleanse us of the works of evil. Jesus, who died and rose! Jesus, the Lord! Dear brothers and sisters, God does not let us die in our sins. Even when we turn our backs on him, he never leaves us to our own devices. He seeks us out, runs after us, to call us to repentance and to cleanse us of our sins. "As I live, says the Lord, I have no pleasure in the death of the wicked, but that the wicked turn from his way and live" (Ezek 33:11). The Lord wants us to be saved and to become living temples of his love, in fraternity, in service, in mercy.

Jesus not only cleanses us of our sins, but he also gives us a share in his own power and wisdom. He liberates us from the narrow and divisive notions of family, faith, and community that divide, oppose, and exclude, so that we can build a Church and a society open to everyone and concerned for our brothers and sisters in greatest need. At the same time, he strengthens us to resist the temptation to seek revenge, which only plunges us into a spiral of endless retaliation. In the power of the Holy Spirit, he sends us forth, not as proselytizers, but as missionary disciples, men and women called to testify to the life-changing power of the Gospel. The risen Lord makes us instruments of God's mercy and peace, patient and courageous artisans of a new social order. In this way, by the power of Christ and the Holy Spirit, the prophetic words of the Apostle Paul to the Corinthians are fulfilled: "God's foolishness is wiser than human wisdom, and God's wisdom is stronger than human strength" (1 Cor 1:25). Christian communities made up of simple and lowly people become a sign of the coming of his kingdom, a kingdom of love, justice, and peace.

"Destroy this temple, and in three days I will raise it up" (Jn 2:19). Jesus was speaking about the temple of his body, and about the Church as well. The Lord promises us that, by the power of the resurrection, he can raise us, and our communities, from the ruins left by injustice, division, and hatred. That is the promise we celebrate in this Eucharist. With the eyes of faith, we recognize the presence of the crucified and risen Lord in our midst. And we learn to embrace his liberating wisdom, to rest in his wounds, and to find healing and strength to serve the coming of his kingdom in our world. By his wounds, we have been healed (see 1 Pet 2:24). In those wounds, dear brothers and sisters, we find the balm of his merciful love. For he, like the Good Samaritan of humanity, wants to anoint every hurt, to heal every painful memory, and to inspire a future of peace and fraternity in this land.

Homily
Erbil
March 7, 2021

A Better World

When the Seed Dies, It Bears Much Fruit

Today is the day I keep in my heart, that February 15th of 2015. I hold in my heart that baptism of blood, those twenty-one men baptized as Christians with water and the Spirit, and that day also baptized with blood. They are our Saints, Saints of all Christians, Saints of all Christian denominations and traditions. They are those who made their lives white in the blood of the Lamb, they are those ... of the people of God, the faithful people of God.

They had gone to work abroad to support their families: ordinary men, fathers of families, men with the dream [desire] to have children; men with the dignity of workers, who not only seek to bring home bread, but to bring it home with the dignity of work. And these men bore witness to Jesus Christ. Their throats slit by the brutality of ISIS, they died uttering, "Lord Jesus!" confessing the name of Jesus.

It is true that this was a tragedy, that these people lost their lives on the beach; but it is also true that the beach was blessed by their blood. And it is even truer that from their simplicity, from their simple but consistent faith, they received the greatest gift a Christian can receive: bearing witness to Jesus Christ to the point of giving their life.

I thank God our Father because he gave us these courageous brothers. I thank the Holy Spirit because he gave them the strength and consistency to confess Jesus Christ to the point of shedding their blood. I thank the bishops, the priests of the Coptic sister Church that raised them and taught them to grow in the faith. And I thank the mothers of these people, of these twenty-one men, who "nursed" them in the faith: they are the mothers of God's holy people who transmit the faith "in dialect," a dialect that goes beyond languages, the dialect of belonging.

I join all of you, brother bishops, in this commemoration. To you, great, beloved Tawadros, brother bishop and friend. To you, Justin Welby, who also wished to come to this meeting. And to all the other bishops and priests, but above all I join the holy faithful People of God who in their simplicity, with their consistency and inconsistencies, with their graces and sins, carry forth the confession of Jesus Christ: Jesus Christ is Lord.

I thank you, twenty-one Saints, Christian Saints of all confessions, for your witness. And I thank you, Lord Jesus Christ, for being so close to your people, for not forgetting them.

Let us pray together today in memory of these twenty-one Coptic martyrs: may they intercede for us all before the Father. Amen.

Video message in memory
of the Coptic martyrs killed in Libya
February 15, 2021

Peace Is a Gift

We do not have weapons. We believe, however, in the
meek and humble strength of prayer. On this day, the
thirst for peace has become a prayer to God, that wars,
terrorism, and violence may end. The peace that we invoke
from Assisi is not simply a protest against war, nor is it
"a result of negotiations, political compromises or economic bargaining. It is the result of prayer" (John Paul II,
Address, October 27, 1986). We seek in God, who is the
source of communion, the clear waters of peace for which
humanity thirsts: these waters do not flow from the des-
erts of pride and personal interests, from the dry earth of
profit at any cost and the arms trade.

Our religious traditions are diverse. But our differences are not the cause of conflict and dispute, or a cold
distance between us. We have not prayed against one
another today, as has unfortunately sometimes occurred in
history. Without syncretism or relativism, we have rather
prayed side by side and for each other. In this very place
Saint John Paul II said, "More perhaps than ever before in
history, the intrinsic link between an authentic religious
attitude and the great good of peace has become evident to
all." Continuing the journey that began thirty years ago in
Assisi, where the memory of that man of God and of peace
who was Saint Francis remains alive, "once again, gathered
here together, we declare that whoever uses religion to
foment violence contradicts religion's deepest and truest
inspiration" (John Paul II, *Address to Representatives of
the World Religions*, Assisi, January 24, 2002). We further

declare that violence in all its forms does not represent "the true nature of religion. It is the antithesis of religion and contributes to its destruction" (Benedict XVI, *Address*, Assisi, October 27, 2011). We never tire of repeating that the name of God cannot be used to justify violence. Peace alone is holy. Peace alone is holy, not war!

Today we have pleaded for the holy gift of peace. We have prayed that consciences will be mobilized to defend the sacredness of human life, to promote peace between peoples, and to care for creation, our common home. Prayer and concrete acts of cooperation help us to break free from the logic of conflict and to reject the rebellious attitudes of those who know only how to protest and be angry. Prayer and the desire to work together commit us to a true peace that is not illusory: not the calm of one who avoids difficulties and turns away, if his personal interests are not at risk; it is not the cynicism of one who washes his hands of any problem that is not his; it is not the virtual approach of one who judges everything and everyone using a computer keyboard, without opening his eyes to the needs of his brothers and sisters, and dirtying his hands for those in need. Our path leads us to immersing ourselves in situations and giving first place to those who suffer; to taking on conflicts and healing them from within; to following ways of goodness with consistency, rejecting the shortcuts offered by evil; to patiently engaging processes of peace, in goodwill and with God's help.

Peace, a thread of hope that unites earth to heaven, a word so simple and difficult at the same time. Peace means *Forgiveness*, the fruit of conversion and prayer, that is born

from within and that, in God's name, makes it possible
to heal old wounds. Peace means *Welcome*, openness to
dialogue, the overcoming of closed-mindedness, which is
not a strategy for safety, but rather a bridge over an empty
space. Peace means *Cooperation*, a concrete and active
exchange with another, who is a gift and not a problem, a
brother or sister with whom to build a better world. Peace
denotes *Education*, a call to learn every day the challenging
art of communion, to acquire a culture of encounter, puri-
fying the conscience of every temptation to violence and
stubbornness which are contrary to the name of God and
human dignity.

> *Address to representatives of churches,*
> *Christian communities, and religions*
> *Assisi*
> *September 20, 2016*

There Is No Alternative to Peace

Encounter and unity are always to be sought, without fear
of diversity. So it is with peace: it too must be cultivated
in the parched soil of conflict and discord, because today,
in spite of everything, there is no real alternative to peacemaking. Truces maintained by walls and displays of power
will not lead to peace, but only the concrete desire to listen
and to engage in dialogue. We commit ourselves to walking, praying, and working together, in the hope that the
art of encounter will prevail over strategies of conflict—in

the hope that the display of threatening *signs of power* will yield to the *power of signs*: men and women of goodwill of different beliefs, unafraid of dialogue, open to the ideas of others and concerned for their good. Only in this way, by ensuring that no one lacks bread and work, dignity and hope, will the cries of war turn into songs of peace.

Address at the Conclusion of the Dialogue
Bari, Italy
July 7, 2018

Peace Comes from the Cross

Everyone who follows Christ receives true peace, the peace that Christ alone can give, a peace that the world cannot give. Many people, when they think of Saint Francis, think of peace; very few people, however, go deeper. What is the peace that Francis received, experienced, and lived, and which he passes on to us? It is the peace of Christ, which is born of the greatest love of all, the love of the cross. It is the peace that the risen Jesus gave to his disciples when he stood in their midst (see Jn 20:19–20).

Franciscan peace is not something saccharine. Hardly! That is not the real Saint Francis! Nor is it a kind of pantheistic harmony with forces of the cosmos. . . . That is not Franciscan either! It is not Franciscan, but a notion that some people have invented! The peace of Saint Francis is the peace of Christ, and it is found by those who "take up" their "yoke," namely, Christ's commandment: love one another as I have loved you (see Jn 13:34; 15:12). This yoke cannot be borne with arrogance, presumption, or pride, but only with meekness and humbleness of heart.

We turn to you, Francis, and we ask you: teach us to be "instruments of peace," of that peace that has its source in God, the peace that Jesus has brought.

Homily
Assisi
October 4, 2013

True Peace Costs

Before leaving, the Lord greets his followers and gives the gift of peace (see Jn 14:27–31), the Lord's peace: "Peace I leave with you; my peace I give to you. Not as the world gives do I give it to you. Do not let your hearts be troubled or afraid" (v. 27). It is not universal peace—that peace without wars that we all want there to be forever—but the peace of the heart, the peace of the soul, the peace that each one of us has inside. And the Lord gives it, but, he emphasizes, "not as the world gives" (v. 27). How does the world give peace, and how does the Lord give it? Are they different forms of peace? Yes.

The world gives you "inner peace"—we are talking about this, peace in your life, living with your "heart at peace"—it gives you inner peace as if it were *your own possession*, like something that is yours and isolates you from others, that you keep for yourself, a personal acquisition: I am at peace. And without realizing it you close yourself up in that peace. It is a peace that is only for you, for each person; it is a solitary peace, it is a peace that makes you serene, even happy. And in this tranquility, in this happiness, it can lull you to sleep; it anesthetizes you and makes you stay within yourself in a certain tranquility. It is a bit selfish: peace for me, closed up in myself. This is how the world gives it to you (see v. 27). It is a costly peace, because you must continually change the "instruments of peace": when you are enthusiastic about something, one thing gives you peace; then it ends and you have to find another. It is costly because it is *temporary* and *sterile*.

Instead, the peace that Jesus gives is another thing. It is a peace that puts you *in motion*: it does not isolate you. It puts you in motion, it makes you go toward others, it creates community, it creates communication. The world's peace is costly, whereas Jesus's is freely given, it is free; it is a gift from the Lord, the peace of the Lord. It is fruitful, it always leads you forward.

An example from the Gospel that makes me think of what the world's peace is like is that man whose barns were full and whose harvest that year seemed to be very big, and thought, "I must build other warehouses, other barns to put this in, and then I will be fine. . . . This is my tranquility, this way I can live serenely." "You fool," says God, "this night your life will be demanded of you" (see Lk 12:13–21). It is a temporary peace that does not open the door to the hereafter. Instead the Lord's peace opens to the place where he went, it is open to Heaven, it is open to Paradise. It is a fruitful peace that is open and brings others with you as well to Paradise.

I think that it would help us to think a bit: What kind of peace do I have? Where do I find peace? In things, in well-being, in travel—but nowadays one cannot travel—in possessions, in many things, or do I find peace as a gift from the Lord? Must I *pay* for peace, or do I receive it freely from the Lord? What kind of peace do I have? When I am missing something, do I get angry? This is not the Lord's peace. This is one of the tests. Am I calm in my peace, do I get "lulled to sleep"? It is not the Lord's. Am I in peace and do I want to communicate it to others, do I want to accomplish something? That is the Lord's peace! Even in bad or difficult moments, does that peace remain in me? It is the Lord's. And the Lord's peace is *fruitful* for me too, because it is full of hope—that is, it looks toward Heaven.

Yesterday—excuse me if I say these things, but they are things about life that are good for me—yesterday I received a letter from a priest, a good priest. And he said to me that I speak little about Heaven. I should speak about it more. And he is right, he is right. And because of this, I wanted to emphasize it today. That the peace Jesus gives us is a peace for today and for the future. It is beginning to live Heaven, with the fruitfulness of Heaven. It is not anesthesia. The other peace is: you anesthetize yourself with things of the world, and when the dose of this anesthetic wears off, you take another one, and another. . . . This peace [of Jesus] is a *definitive* peace, fruitful and "contagious." It is not narcissistic, because it always looks to the Lord. The other form of peace is about looking at yourself; it is a bit narcissistic.

May the Lord give us this peace, full of hope, that makes us fruitful, that makes us communicative with others, that creates community, and that always looks to the definitive peace of Paradise.

Homily
Chapel of the Casa Santa Marta
May 12, 2020

Nonviolence: A Style of Politics for Peace

This is the fiftieth Message for the World Day of Peace.... On this occasion, I would like to reflect on *nonviolence* as a style of politics for peace. I ask God to help all of us to cultivate nonviolence in our most personal thoughts and values. May charity and nonviolence govern how we treat each other as individuals, within society and in international life. When victims of violence are able to resist the temptation to retaliate, they become the most credible promoters of nonviolent peacemaking. In the most local and ordinary situations and in the international order, may nonviolence become the hallmark of our decisions, our relationships, and our actions, and indeed of political life in all its forms.

While the last century knew the devastation of two deadly world wars, the threat of nuclear war, and a great number of other conflicts, today, sadly, we find ourselves engaged in a horrifying *world war fought piecemeal.* It is not easy to know if our world is presently more or less violent than in the past, or to know whether modern means of communications and greater mobility have made us more aware of violence, or, on the other hand, increasingly inured to it.

In any case, we know that this piecemeal violence, of different kinds and levels, causes great suffering: wars in different countries and continents; terrorism, organized crime, and unforeseen acts of violence; the abuses suffered by migrants and victims of human trafficking; and the devastation of the environment. Where does this lead? Can violence achieve any goal of lasting value? Or does it merely lead to retaliation and a cycle of deadly conflicts that benefit only a few "warlords"?

Violence is not the cure for our broken world. . . .

Jesus himself lived in violent times. Yet he taught that the true battlefield, where violence and peace meet, is the human heart: for "it is from within, from the human heart, that evil intentions come" (Mk 7:21). But Christ's message in this regard offers a radically positive approach. He unfailingly preached God's unconditional love, which welcomes and forgives. He taught his disciples to love their enemies (see Mt 5:44) and to turn the other cheek (see Mt 5:39). When he stopped her accusers from stoning the woman caught in adultery (see Jn 8:1–11), and when, on the night before he died, he told Peter to put away his sword (see Mt 26:52), Jesus marked out the path of non-violence. He walked that path to the very end, to the cross, whereby he became our peace and put an end to hostility (see Eph 2:14–16). Whoever accepts the Good News of Jesus is able to acknowledge the violence within and be healed by God's mercy, becoming in turn an instrument of reconciliation. In the words of Saint Francis of Assisi, "As you announce peace with your mouth, make sure that you have greater peace in your hearts."

To be true followers of Jesus today also includes embracing his teaching about nonviolence. As my predecessor Benedict XVI observed, that teaching "is realistic because it takes into account that in the world there is *too much* violence, *too much* injustice, and therefore that this situation cannot be overcome except by countering it with *more* love, with *more* goodness. This '*more*' comes from God" (Angelus, February 18, 2007). He went on to stress, "For Christians, nonviolence is not merely tactical behavior but a person's way of being, the attitude of one who is *so convinced of God's love and power* that he or she is not afraid to tackle evil with the weapons of love and truth alone. Love of one's enemy constitutes the nucleus of the 'Christian revolution.'" The Gospel command to *love your enemies* (see Lk 6:27) "is rightly considered the *magna carta* of Christian nonviolence. It does not consist in succumbing to evil . . . , but in responding to evil with good (see Rom 12:17–21), and thereby breaking the chain of injustice."

The decisive and consistent practice of nonviolence has produced impressive results. The achievements of Mahatma Gandhi and Abdul Ghaffar Khan in the liberation of India, and of Dr. Martin Luther King Jr. in combating racial discrimination will never be forgotten. Women in particular are often leaders of nonviolence, as, for example, were Leymah Gbowee and the thousands of Liberian women who organized pray-ins and nonviolent protests that resulted in high-level peace talks to end the second civil war in Liberia.

Nor can we forget the eventful decade that ended with the fall of Communist regimes in Europe. The Christian communities made their own contribution by their insistent prayer and courageous action. Particularly influential were the ministry and teaching of Saint John Paul II. Reflecting on the events of 1989 in his 1991 encyclical *Centesimus Annus*, my predecessor highlighted the fact that momentous change in the lives of people, nations, and states had come about "by means of peaceful protest, using only the weapons of truth and justice." This peaceful political transition was made possible in part "by the nonviolent commitment of people who, while always refusing to yield to the force of power, succeeded time after time in finding effective ways of bearing witness to the truth." Pope John Paul went on to say, "May people learn to fight for justice without violence, renouncing class struggle in their internal disputes and war in international ones" (*CA* 23).

Peacebuilding through active nonviolence is the natural and necessary complement to the Church's continuing efforts to limit the use of force by the application of moral norms; she does so by her participation in the work of international institutions and through the competent contribution made by so many Christians to the drafting of legislation at all levels. Jesus himself offers a "manual" for this strategy of peacemaking in the Sermon on the Mount. The eight Beatitudes (see Mt 5:3–10) provide a portrait of the person we could describe as blessed, good, and authentic. Blessed are the meek, Jesus tells us, the merciful and the peacemakers, those who are pure in heart, and those who hunger and thirst for justice.

This is also a program and a challenge for political and religious leaders, the heads of international institutions, and business and media executives: to apply the Beatitudes in the exercise of their respective responsibilities. It is a challenge to build up society, communities, and businesses by acting as peacemakers. It is to show mercy by refusing to discard people, harm the environment, or seek to win at any cost. To do so requires "the willingness to face conflict head on, to resolve it and to make it a link in the chain of a new process" (*Evangelii Gaudium* 227). To act in this way means to choose solidarity as a way of making history and building friendship in society. Active nonviolence is a way of showing that unity is truly more powerful and more fruitful than conflict. Everything in the world is interconnected. Certainly differences can cause frictions. But let us face them constructively and nonviolently, so that "tensions and oppositions can achieve a diversified and life-giving unity," preserving "what is valid and useful on both sides" (227).

Mary is the Queen of Peace. At the birth of her Son, the angels gave glory to God and wished peace on earth to men and women of goodwill (see Luke 2:14). Let us pray for her guidance.

All of us want peace. Many people build it day by day through small gestures and acts; many of them are suffering, yet patiently persevere in their efforts to be peacemakers. May we dedicate ourselves prayerfully and actively to banishing violence from our hearts, words, and deeds, and to becoming nonviolent people and to building nonviolent communities that care for our common home. Nothing is impossible if we turn to God in prayer. Everyone can be an artisan of peace.

Message for the Fiftieth World Day of Peace
January 1, 2017

An Artisanal Path

Peace Is a Path

Setting out on a journey of peace is a challenge made all the more complex because the interests at stake in relationships between people, communities, and nations are numerous and conflicting. We must first appeal to people's moral conscience and to personal and political will. Peace emerges from the depths of the human heart, and political will must always be renewed so that new ways can be found to reconcile and unite individuals and communities.

The world does not need empty words but convinced witnesses, peacemakers who are open to a dialogue that rejects exclusion or manipulation. In fact, we cannot truly achieve peace without a convinced dialogue between men and women who seek the truth beyond ideologies and differing opinions. Peace "must be built up continually" (*Gaudium et Spes*, 78); it is a journey made together in constant pursuit of the common good, truthfulness, and respect for law. Listening to one another can lead to mutual understanding and esteem, and even to seeing in an enemy the face of a brother or sister.

The peace process thus requires enduring commitment. It is a patient effort to seek truth and justice, to honor the memory of victims, and to open the way, step by step, to a shared hope stronger than the desire for vengeance. In a state based on law, democracy can be an important paradigm of this process, provided it is grounded in justice and a commitment to protect the rights of every person, especially the weak and marginalized, in a constant search for truth. This is a social undertaking, an ongoing work in which each individual makes his or her contribution responsibly, at every level of the local, national, and global community.

As Saint Paul VI pointed out, these "two aspirations, to equality and to participation, seek to promote a democratic society. . . . This calls for an education to social life, involving not only the knowledge of each person's rights, but also its necessary correlative: the recognition of his or her duties with regard to others. The sense and practice of duty are themselves conditioned by the capacity for self-mastery and by the acceptance of responsibility and of the limits placed upon the freedom of individuals or the groups" (*Octogesima Adveniens*, 24).

Divisions within a society, the increase of social inequalities, and the refusal to employ the means of ensuring integral human development endanger the pursuit of the common good. Yet patient efforts based on the power of the word and of truth can help foster a greater capacity for compassion and creative solidarity.

In our Christian experience, we constantly remember Christ, who gave his life to reconcile us to one another (see Rom 5:6–11). The Church shares fully in the search for a just social order; she continues to serve the common good and to nourish the hope for peace by transmitting Christian values and moral teaching, and by her social and educational works.

The Bible, especially in the words of the Prophets, reminds individuals and peoples of God's covenant with humanity, which entails renouncing our desire to dominate others and learning to see one another as persons, sons and daughters of God, brothers and sisters. We should never encapsulate others in what they may have said or done, but value them for the promise that they embody. Only by choosing the path of respect can we break the spiral of vengeance and set out on the journey of hope.

We are guided by the Gospel passage that tells of the following conversation between Peter and Jesus: "Lord, how often shall my brother sin against me, and I forgive him? As many as seven times?" Jesus said to him, "I do not say to you seven times, but seventy times seven" (Mt 18:21–22). This path of reconciliation is a summons to discover in the depths of our heart the power of forgiveness and the capacity to acknowledge one another as brothers and sisters. When we learn to live in forgiveness, we grow in our capacity to become men and women of peace.

What is true of peace in a social context is also true in the areas of politics and the economy, since peace permeates every dimension of life in common. There can be no true peace unless we show ourselves capable of developing a more just economic system. As Pope Benedict XVI said ten years ago in his Encyclical Letter *Caritas in Veritate*, "In order to defeat underdevelopment, action is required not only on improving exchange-based transactions and implanting public welfare structures, but above all on gradually increasing openness, in a world context, to forms of economic activity marked by quotas of gratuitousness and communion" (no. 39).

The journey of reconciliation calls for patience and trust. Peace will not be obtained unless it is hoped for.

In the first place, this means believing in the possibility of peace, believing that others need peace just as much as we do. Here we can find inspiration in the love that God has for each of us: a love that is liberating, limitless, gratuitous, and tireless.

Fear is frequently a source of conflict. So it is important to overcome our human fears and acknowledge that we are needy children in the eyes of the One who loves us and awaits us, like the father of the prodigal son (see Lk 15:11–24). The culture of fraternal encounter shatters the culture of conflict. It makes of every encounter a possibility and a gift of God's generous love. It leads us beyond the limits of our narrow horizons and constantly encourages us to a live in a spirit of universal fraternity, as children of the one heavenly Father.

Message for the LIII World Day of Peace
January 1, 2020

Peace Is Daily

Peace is not a document that gets signed and then filed away. Peace is built day by day! And peace is crafted; it is the work of our hands; it is built up by the way we live our lives. But someone may say, "Tell me, Father, how can I build peace? How can I be a peacemaker?" First: Never hate anyone. If someone wrongs you, seek to forgive. No hatred! Much forgiveness! Let us all say this together: "No hatred! Much forgiveness!" [*All repeat in Sango.*] And if hatred does not dwell in your heart, if you forgive, then you will be a winner. Because you will win the hardest battle in life; you will win in love. And from love comes peace.

> *Homily during the prayer vigil*
> *Bangui (Central African Republic)*
> *November 29, 2015*

Dialogue Opens the Way

Social peace demands hard work, craftsmanship. It would be easier to keep freedoms and differences in check with cleverness and a few resources. But such a peace would be superficial and fragile, not the fruit of a culture of encounter that brings enduring stability. Integrating differences is a much more difficult and slow process, yet it is the guarantee of a genuine and lasting peace. That peace is not achieved by recourse only to those who are pure and untainted, since "even people who can be considered questionable on account of their errors have something to offer which must not be overlooked" (*Evangelii Gaudium*, 236). Nor does it come from ignoring social demands or quelling disturbances, since it is not "a consensus on paper or a transient peace for a contented minority" (208). What is important is to create *processes* of encounter, processes that build a people that can accept differences. Let us arm our children with the weapons of dialogue! Let us teach them to fight the good fight of the culture of encounter!

Fratelli tutti, 217

Pray for Those Who Do Not Love Us

It can be done with simplicity. Perhaps the rancor remains; perhaps the resentment remains in us, but we are making the effort to follow the path of this God who is so good, merciful, holy, and perfect that he makes his sun rise on the bad and the good: he is for everyone, he is good for everyone. We must be good to everyone. And pray for those who are not good, for everyone.

Do we pray for those who kill children in war? It is difficult, it's a long way off, but we have to learn to do it, for them to be converted. Do we pray for those people who are closest to us and hate us or hurt us? "Eh, Father, it's hard! I would want to wring their necks!"—Pray. Pray that the Lord changes their lives. Prayer is an antidote against hatred, against wars, these wars that begin at home, that begin in the neighborhood, that begin in families. . . . Just think of the wars in families over inheritance: how many families are destroyed. They hate each other because of inheritance. Pray for peace. And if I know that someone does not love me well, does not love me, I must pray especially for him. Prayer is powerful, prayer defeats evil, prayer brings peace.

Homily
Castelverde di Lunghezza (Rome)
February 19, 2017

Learning the Art of Dialogue

To build a new world, a better world, every kind of cruelty must be eradicated. And war is cruelty. But this type of war is even crueler because it rages against those who are innocent.

Then, to listen to the other person, the capacity to listen, not to argue immediately, to ask—and this means dialogue, and dialogue is a bridge. Dialogue is a bridge. Do not be afraid to dialogue. Now this is not about the San Lorenzo–Lanus match, which is being played today—we shall see who wins. It is about agreeing to proposals so as to move forward together. Everyone wins in dialogue; no one loses. In an argument, one wins and the other loses or both lose. Dialogue is gentleness, the capacity to listen; it is to put oneself in the other's place, it is to form a bridge, and within the dialogue, if I have a different opinion, not to argue, but rather to seek to persuade with gentleness.

Words at the World Congress
of the Pontifical Foundation "Scholas occurrentes"
New Synod Hall
May 29, 2016

Architecture of Reconciliation

Negotiation often becomes necessary for shaping concrete paths to peace. Yet the processes of change that lead to lasting peace are crafted above all by peoples; each individual can act as an effective leaven by the way he or she lives each day. Great changes are not produced behind desks or in offices. This means that everyone has a fundamental role to play in a single great creative project: to write a new page of history, a page full of hope, peace, and reconciliation. There is an "architecture" of peace, to which different institutions of society contribute, each according to its own area of expertise, but there is also an "art" of peace that involves us all. From the various peace processes that have taken place in different parts of the world, we have learned that these ways of making peace, of placing reason above revenge, of the delicate harmony between politics and law, cannot ignore the involvement of ordinary people. Peace is not achieved by normative frameworks and institutional arrangements between well-meaning political or economic groups. . . . It is always helpful to incorporate into our peace processes the experience of those sectors that have often been overlooked, so that communities themselves can influence the development of a collective memory.

Fratelli tutti, 231

Overcoming Evil with Good

To be sure, it is no easy task to overcome the bitter legacy of injustices, hostility, and mistrust left by conflict. It can only be done by overcoming evil with good (see Rom 12:21) and by cultivating those virtues that foster reconciliation, solidarity, and peace. In this way, persons who nourish goodness in their heart find that such goodness leads to a peaceful conscience and to profound joy, even in the midst of difficulties and misunderstandings. Even when affronted, goodness is never weak, but rather shows its strength by refusing to take revenge. Each of us should realize that even the harsh judgment I hold in my heart against my brother or my sister, the open wound that was never cured, the offense that was never forgiven, the rancor that is only going to hurt me, are all instances of a struggle that I carry within me, a little flame deep in my heart that needs to be extinguished before it turns into a great blaze.

Fratelli tutti, 243

Peace Is the Priority

The commandment of peace is inscribed in the depths of the religious traditions. Believers have understood that religious differences do not justify indifference or enmity. Rather, on the basis of our religious faith we are enabled to become peacemakers, rather than standing passively before the evil of war and hatred. Religions stand at the service of peace and fraternity. For this reason, our present gathering also represents an incentive to religious leaders and to all believers to pray fervently for peace, never resigned to war, but working with the gentle strength of faith to end conflicts.

We need peace! More peace! We cannot remain indifferent. Today the world has a profound thirst for peace. In many countries, people are suffering due to wars that, though often forgotten, are always the cause of suffering and poverty. The world, political life, and public opinion all run the risk of growing inured to the evil of war, as if it were simply a part of human history.

"Let us not remain mired in theoretical discussions, but touch the wounded flesh of the victims. . . . Let us think of the refugees and displaced, those who suffered the effects of atomic radiation and chemical attacks, the mothers who lost their children, and the boys and girls maimed or deprived of their childhood" (*Fratelli tutti*, 261). Today the sufferings of war are aggravated by the suffering caused by the coronavirus and the impossibility, in many countries, of access to necessary care.

In the meantime, conflicts continue, bringing in their wake suffering and death. To put an end to war is a solemn duty before God incumbent on all those holding political responsibilities. Peace is the priority of all politics. God will ask an accounting of those who failed to seek peace, or who fomented tensions and conflicts. He will call them to account for all the days, months, and years of war that have passed and been endured by the world's peoples!

The words of the Lord Jesus are incisive and full of wisdom: "Put your sword back into its place; for all who take the sword will perish by the sword" (Mt 26:52). Those who wield the sword, possibly in the belief that it will resolve difficult situations quickly, will know in their own lives, the lives of their loved ones, and the lives of their countries the death brought by the sword. "Enough!" says Jesus (Lk 22:38), when his disciples produce two swords before the Passion. "Enough!" That is his unambiguous response to any form of violence. That single word of Jesus echoes through the centuries and reaches us forcefully in our own time: enough of swords, weapons, violence, and war!

Saint Paul VI echoed that in his appeal to the United Nations in 1965: "No more war!" This is our plea, and that of all men and women of goodwill. It is the dream of all who strive to work for peace in the realization that "every war leaves our world worse than it was before" (*Fratelli tutti*, 261).

How do we find a way out of intransigent and festering conflicts? How do we untangle the knots of so many armed struggles? How do we prevent conflicts? How do we inspire thoughts of peace in warlords and those who rely on the strength of arms? No people, no social group can *single-handedly* achieve peace, prosperity, security, and happiness. None. The lesson learned from the recent pandemic, if we wish to be honest, is "the awareness that we are a global community, all in the same boat, where one person's problems are the problems of all. Once more we realized that no one is saved alone; we can only be saved together" (*Fratelli tutti*, 32).

Fraternity, born of the realization that we are a single human family, must penetrate the life of peoples, communities, government leaders, and international assemblies. This will help everyone to understand that we can only be saved together through encounter and negotiation, setting aside our conflicts and pursuing reconciliation, moderating the language of politics and propaganda, and developing true paths of peace (see *Fratelli tutti*, 231).

We have gathered this evening, as persons of different religious traditions, in order to send a message of peace. To show clearly that the religions do not want war and, indeed, disown those who would enshrine violence, that they ask everyone to pray for reconciliation and to strive to enable fraternity to pave new paths of hope. For indeed, with God's help, it will be possible to build a world of peace, and thus, brothers and sisters, to be saved together.

> *Address to the International Prayer Meeting for Peace*
> *Piazza del Campidoglio*
> *October 20, 2020*

Ecological Conversion

Faced with the consequences of our hostility toward others, our lack of respect for our common home, or our abusive exploitation of natural resources—seen only as a source of immediate profit, regardless of local communities, the common good, and nature itself—we are in need of an ecological conversion. The recent Synod on the Pan-Amazon region moves us to make a pressing renewed call for a peaceful relationship between communities and the land, between present and past, between experience and hope.

This journey of reconciliation also calls for listening to and contemplation of the world that God has given us as a gift to make our common home. Indeed, natural resources, the many forms of life, and the earth itself have been entrusted to us "to till and keep" (Gen 1:15), also for future generations, through the responsible and active participation of everyone. We need to change the way we think and see things, and to become more open to encountering others and accepting the gift of creation, which reflects the beauty and wisdom of its Creator.

All this gives us deeper motivation and a new way to dwell in our common home, to accept our differences, to respect and celebrate the life that we have received and share, and to seek living conditions and models of society that favor the continued flourishing of life and the development of the common good of the entire human family.

The ecological conversion for which we are appealing will lead us to a new way of looking at life, as we consider the generosity of the Creator who has given us the earth and called us to share it in joy and moderation. This conversion must be understood in an integral way, as a transformation of how we relate to our sisters and brothers, to other living beings, to creation in all its rich variety, and to the Creator who is the origin and source of all life. For Christians, it requires that "the effects of their encounter with Jesus Christ become evident in their relationship with the world around them" (*Laudato si'*, 217).

Message for the LIII World Day of Peace
January 1, 2020

Brothers and Sisters

In the name of God who has created all human beings equal
in rights, duties, and dignity, and who has called them to live
together as brothers and sisters, to fill the earth and make
known the values of goodness, love, and peace;

In the name of innocent human life that God has for-
bidden to kill, affirming that whoever kills a person is like
one who kills the whole of humanity, and that whoever saves
a person is like one who saves the whole of humanity;

In the name of the poor, the destitute, the marginalized, and those most in need whom God has commanded
us to help as a duty required of all persons, especially the
wealthy and of means;

In the name of orphans, widows, refugees, and those
exiled from their homes and their countries; in the name
of all victims of wars, persecution, and injustice; in the
name of the weak, those who live in fear, prisoners of
war, and those tortured in any part of the world, without
distinction;

In the name of peoples who have lost their security,
peace, and the possibility of living together, becoming victims of destruction, calamity, and war;

In the name of *human fraternity* that embraces all
human beings, unites them, and renders them equal;

In the name of this *fraternity* torn apart by policies of
extremism and division, by systems of unrestrained profit
or by hateful ideological tendencies that manipulate the
actions and the future of men and women;

In the name of freedom, that God has given to all human beings, creating them free and distinguishing them by this gift;

In the name of justice and mercy, the foundations of prosperity and the cornerstone of faith;

In the name of all persons of goodwill present in every part of the world;

In the name of God and of everything stated thus far; Al-Azhar al-Sharif and the Muslims of the East and West, together with the Catholic Church and the Catholics of the East and West, declare the adoption of a culture of dialogue as the path; mutual cooperation as the code of conduct; reciprocal understanding as the method and standard.

We, who believe in God and all of this . . . we call upon ourselves, upon the leaders of the world as well as the architects of international policy and world economy, to work strenuously to spread the culture of tolerance and of living together in peace; to intervene at the earliest opportunity to stop the shedding of innocent blood and bring an end to wars, conflicts, environmental decay, and the moral and cultural decline that the world is presently experiencing. . . .

Moreover, we resolutely declare that religions must never incite war, hateful attitudes, hostility, and extremism, nor must they incite violence or the shedding of blood. These tragic realities are the consequence of a deviation from religious teachings. They result from a political manipulation of religions and from interpretations made by religious groups who, in the course of history, have taken advantage of the power of religious sentiment in the hearts of men and women in order to make them act in a way that has nothing to do with the truth of religion. This is done for the purpose of achieving objectives that are political, economic, worldly, and shortsighted. We thus call upon all concerned to stop using religions to incite hatred, violence, extremism, and blind fanaticism, and to refrain from using the name of God to justify acts of murder, exile, terrorism, and oppression. We ask this on the basis of our common belief in God, who did not create men and women to be killed or to fight one another, nor to be tortured or humiliated in their lives and circumstances. God, the Almighty, has no need to be defended by anyone and does not want his name to be used to terrorize people.

From the Document on Human Brotherhood
Abu Dhabi
February 4, 2019
Signed by Pope Francis as well as
the Grand Imam of al-Azhar, Ahmed el-Tayeb

Fraternity Is the Grace of God the Father

As he says farewell to his disciples (see Jn 14:15–21), Jesus gives them tranquility. He gives peace, with a promise: "I will not leave you orphans" (v. 18). He defends them from that pain, from that painful feeling of being orphans. In today's world, there is a great *sense of being orphaned*: many people have many things, but they lack the Father. And in the history of humanity, this has repeated itself: when the Father is missing, something is lacking and there is always the desire to meet, to rediscover the Father, even in the ancient myths. We can think of the myth of Oedipus, or Telemachus, and many others: always in search of the Father who is missing. Today we can say that we live in a society where the Father is missing, a sense of being orphaned that specifically affects belonging and fraternity.

And so Jesus promises, "I will ask the Father and he will give you another Paraclete" (v. 16). Jesus says, "I am going away, but someone else will come who will teach you how to *access the Father*. He will remind you how to access the Father." The Holy Spirit does not come to "make us his clients"; he comes to point out how to access the Father, to remind us how to access the Father. That is what Jesus opened, what Jesus showed us. A spirituality of the Son alone or the Holy Spirit alone does not exist: the center is the Father. The Son is sent by the Father and returns to the Father. The Holy Spirit is sent by the Father to remind us and to teach us how to access the Father.

Only with this awareness of being children, that *we are not orphans*, can we live in peace among ourselves. Wars, either small ones or large ones, always have a dimension of being orphans: the Father who makes peace is missing. And so when Peter and the first community respond to the people regarding why they are Christians (see 1 Pt 3:15–18), it says, "Do it with gentleness and reverence, keeping your conscience clear" (v. 16), that is, the gentleness that the Holy Spirit gives. The Holy Spirit teaches us this gentleness, this tenderness of the Father's children. The Holy Spirit does not teach us to *insult*. And one of the consequences of this feeling like orphans is insulting, wars, because if there is no Father, there are no brothers, fraternity is lost. They are—this tenderness, reverence, gentleness—they are attitudes of belonging, of belonging to a family that is certain of having a Father.

"I will pray to the Father and he will send you another Paraclete" (Jn 14:16) who will remind you how to access the Father. He will remind you that we *have a Father* who is the center of everything, the origin of everything, the one who unites everyone, the salvation of everyone because he sent his Son to save everyone. And now he sends the Holy Spirit to remind us how to access him, the Father, and of this paternity, of this fraternal attitude of gentleness, tenderness, and peace.

Let us ask the Holy Spirit to remind us always, always about this access to the Father, that he might remind us that we have a Father. And to this civilization, with this great feeling of being orphaned, may he grant the grace of rediscovering the Father, the Father who gives meaning to all of life, and that he might unite humanity into one family.

Homily
Chapel of Santa Marta House
May 17, 2020

Easter Makes the Encounter with the Other Sprout Up

Fraternity is the fruit of the Easter of Christ who, with his death and Resurrection, conquered sin, which separated man from God, man from himself, man from his brothers. But we know that sin always separates, always creates hostility. Jesus broke down the wall that divides people and restored peace, beginning to weave the fabric of a new fraternity. It is so important in our time to rediscover brotherhood as it was experienced by the early Christian communities, to rediscover how to make room for Jesus who never divides and always unites. There cannot be true communion and commitment to the common good and social justice without fraternity and sharing. Without fraternal sharing, no ecclesial or civil community can be formed: there is only an ensemble of individuals moved or grouped together, according to common interests. But brotherhood is a grace that Jesus creates.

The Easter of Christ has caused another thing to erupt into the world: *the novelty of dialogue and relationship*, a novelty that has become a responsibility for Christians. Jesus in fact said, "By this all men will know that you are my disciples, if you have love for one another" (Jn 13:35). This is why we cannot close ourselves off in our private world, within our group, but instead we are called to safeguard the common good and to take care of our brothers and sisters, in particular those who are weakest and most marginalized. Only fraternity can guarantee a lasting peace, can overcome poverty, can extinguish tension and war, can eradicate corruption and crime. May the Angel who tells us, "He has risen," help us to live the fraternity and the novelty of dialogue and relationships and of concern for the common good.

Words before the Regina Coeli
April 2, 2018

Follow Another Logic

Calvary was the site of a great "duel" between God, who came to save us, and man, who wants to save only himself; between faith in God and worship of self; between man who accuses and God who excuses. In the end, God's victory was revealed; his mercy came down upon the earth. From the cross, forgiveness poured forth and fraternal love was reborn: "the Cross makes us brothers and sisters" (Benedict XVI, *Address at the Way of the Cross at the Colosseum*, March 21, 2008). Jesus's arms, outstretched on the cross, mark the turning point, for God points a finger at no one, but instead embraces all. For love alone extinguishes hatred, love alone can ultimately triumph over injustice. Love alone makes room for others. Love alone is the path toward full communion among us.

Let us look upon the crucified God and ask him to grant us the grace to be more united and more fraternal. When we are tempted to follow the way of this world, may we be reminded of Jesus's words: "Whoever would save his life will lose it; and whoever loses his life for my sake and the Gospel's will save it" (Mk 8:35). What is counted loss in the eyes of the world is, for us, salvation. May we learn from the Lord, who saved us by emptying himself (see Phil 2:7) and *becoming other*: from being God, he became man; from spirit, he became flesh; from a king, he became a slave. He asks us to do the same, to humble ourselves, to "become other" in order to reach out to others. The closer we become to the Lord Jesus, the more we will be open and "universal," since we will feel responsible for others.

And others will become the means of our own salvation: all others, every human person, whatever his or her history and beliefs—beginning with the poor, who are those most like Christ. The great Archbishop of Constantinople, Saint John Chrysostom, once wrote, "If there were no poor, the greater part of our salvation would be overthrown" (*On the Second Letter to the Corinthians* XVII.2). May the Lord help us to journey together on the path of fraternity, and thus to become credible witnesses of the living God.

Homily at the International Prayer Meeting for Peace
Church of Saint Maria in Aracoeli
October 20, 2020

Prayers

A Prayer to the Creator

Lord, Father of our human family,
you created all human beings equal in dignity:
pour forth into our hearts a fraternal spirit
and inspire in us a dream of renewed encounter,
dialogue, justice, and peace.
Move us to create healthier societies
and a more dignified world,
a world without hunger, poverty, violence, and war.
May our hearts be open
to all the peoples and nations of the earth.
May we recognize the goodness and beauty
that you have sown in each of us,
and thus forge bonds of unity, common projects,
and shared dreams. Amen.

Fratelli tutti, 287

An Ecumenical Christian Prayer

> O God, Trinity of love,
> from the profound communion of your divine life,
> pour out upon us a torrent of fraternal love.
> Grant us the love reflected in the actions of Jesus,
> in his family of Nazareth,
> and in the early Christian community.
> Grant that we Christians may live the Gospel,
> discovering Christ in each human being,
> recognizing him crucified
> in the sufferings of the abandoned
> and forgotten of our world,
> and risen in each brother or sister
> who makes a new start.
> Come, Holy Spirit, show us your beauty,
> reflected in all the peoples of the earth,
> so that we may discover anew
> that all are important and all are necessary,
> different faces of the one humanity
> that God so loves. Amen.

Fratelli tutti, 287

Prayer for Fraternity

> Almighty and eternal God,
> good and merciful Father;
> Creator of heaven and earth, of all that is visible
> and invisible;

God of Abraham, God of Isaac, God of Jacob,
King and Lord of the past, of the present, and of
       the future;
sole judge of every man and woman,
who reward your faithful with eternal glory!
We, the descendants of Abraham according to our
       faith in you, the one God,
Jews, Christians, and Muslims,
humbly stand before you
and with trust we pray to you
for this country, Bosnia and Herzegovina,
that men and women, followers of different religions,
       nations, and cultures
may live here in peace and harmony.
We pray to you, O Father,
that it may be so in every country of the world!
Strengthen in each of us faith and hope,
mutual respect and sincere love
for all of our brothers and sisters.
Grant that we may dedicate ourselves
courageously to building a just society,
to being men and women of goodwill,
filled with mutual understanding and forgiveness,
patient artisans of dialogue and peace.
May each of our thoughts, words, and actions
be in harmony with your holy will.

> *From ecumenical and*
> *interreligious meeting*
> *Sarajevo*
> *June 6, 2015*

Prayer of the Children of Abraham

Almighty God, our Creator, you love our human family and every work of your hands:

As children of Abraham, Jews, Christians, and Muslims, together with other believers and all persons of goodwill, we thank you for having given us Abraham, a distinguished son of this noble and beloved country, to be our common father in faith.

We thank you for his example as a man of faith, who obeyed you completely, left behind his family, his tribe, and his native land, and set out for a land that he knew not.

We thank you too, for the example of courage, resilience, strength of spirit, generosity, and hospitality set for us by our common father in faith.

We thank you in a special way for his heroic faith, shown by his readiness even to sacrifice his son in obedience to your command. We know that this was an extreme test, yet one from which he emerged victorious, since he trusted unreservedly in you, who are merciful and always offer the possibility of beginning anew.

We thank you because, in blessing our father Abraham, you made him a blessing for all peoples.

We ask you, the God of our father Abraham and our God, to grant us a strong faith, a faith that abounds in good works, a faith that opens our hearts to you and to all our brothers and sisters; and a boundless hope capable of discerning in every situation your fidelity to your promises.

Make each of us a witness of your loving care for all, particularly refugees and the displaced, widows and orphans, the poor and the infirm.

Open our hearts to mutual forgiveness and in this way make us instruments of reconciliation, builders of a more just and fraternal society.

Welcome into your abode of peace and light all those who have died, particularly the victims of violence and war.

Assist the authorities in the effort to seek and find the victims of kidnapping and in a special way to protect women and children.

Help us to care for the earth, our common home, which in your goodness and generosity you have given to all of us.

From interreligious meeting
Ur Plain
March 6, 2021

Prayer for the Victims of War

Most High God, Lord of all ages, you created the world in love and never cease to shower your blessings upon your creatures. From beyond the sea of suffering and death, from beyond all temptations to violence, injustice, and unjust gain, you accompany your sons and daughters with a Father's tender love.

Yet we men and women, spurning your gifts and absorbed by all-too-worldly concerns, have often forgotten your counsels of peace and harmony. We were concerned

only with ourselves and our narrow interests. Indifferent
to you and to others, we barred the door to peace. What
the prophet Jonah heard said of Nineveh was repeated:
the wickedness of men rose up to heaven (see Jonah 1:2).
We did not lift pure hands to heaven (see 1 Tim 2:8), but
from the earth there arose once more the cry of innocent
blood (see Gen 4:10). In the book of Jonah, the inhabitants of Nineveh heeded the words of your prophet and
found salvation in repentance. Lord, we now entrust to
you the many victims of man's hatred for man. We too
implore your forgiveness and beg the grace of repentance:
Kyrie eleison! Kyrie eleison! Kyrie eleison!

[Brief moment of silence]

Lord our God, in this city, we see two signs of the
perennial human desire for closeness to you: the Al-Nouri
Mosque, with its Al-Hadba minaret, and the Church of
Our Lady of the Hour, whose clock for more than a century has reminded passersby that life is short and that time
is precious. Teach us to realize that you have entrusted to
us your plan of love, peace, and reconciliation, and charged
us to carry it out in our time, in the brief span of our
earthly lives. Make us recognize that only in this way, by
putting it into practice immediately, can this city and this
country be rebuilt, and hearts torn by grief be healed. Help
us not to pass our time in promoting our selfish concerns,
whether as individuals or as groups, but in serving your
loving plan. And whenever we go astray, grant that we
may heed the voice of true men and women of God and

repent in due time, lest we be once more overwhelmed by destruction and death.

To you we entrust all those whose span of earthly life was cut short by the violent hand of their brothers and sisters; we also pray to you for those who caused such harm to their brothers and sisters. May they repent, touched by the power of your mercy.

Eternal rest grant unto them, O Lord, and let perpetual light shine upon them.

May they rest in peace. Amen.

Mosul, Iraq
March 7, 2021

Afterword

A Century-Long Magisterium of Peace

Andrea Tornielli

One cannot understand Francis's "Magisterium of Peace" without placing it in the sequence of papal proclamations of the last century. The lapses in memory and the sheer quantity of information available to us on a daily basis run the risk of making us regard as new or revolutionary attitudes and words imbued with realism and rooted in a solid tradition. In fact, that tradition led the successors of Peter to launch numerous appeals for ceasefires and, step by step, to mark an increasingly clear and resolute rejection of war.

The beginning of this long journey can be traced back to 1848, when the pope still had the Papal States and its own army. At the outbreak of the First War of Independence, in 1848, Pius IX, having initially decided to intervene alongside the Kingdom of Sardinia against Austria, proceed to retrace his steps. In an address on April 29, he pronounced that he could not make war on a Christian people, because as pope he was "father of all the faithful."

With the end of temporal power, the papacy, far from losing its strength, acquired an even greater power, and the pontiff has increasingly become a spiritual and moral authority above all others. Unfortunately, this has not meant that his voice has been heard.

On August 2, 1914, just a few days after the Austro-Hungarian Empire declared war on Serbia following the assassination of Archduke Ferdinand in Sarajevo, Pope Pius X, who would die only a few days later, sent the exhortation *Dum Europa fere omnis* to all Catholics of the world, imploring an end to the conflict. Pope Sarto wrote, "While almost the whole of Europe is being dragged into the whirlpools of a terrible war, whose dangers, massacres, and consequences no one can think of without feeling overwhelmed by pain and fear, we too cannot but be concerned and feel our souls torn by the bitterest pain for the health and lives of so many citizens and peoples that are most dear to our hearts." The "*guerrone*," as Pius X called it, flared up, marking the destinies of Europe throughout the twentieth century.

His successor, Benedict XV, in his letter to the leaders of the belligerent peoples in August 1917, described the Great War as "useless slaughter" and reiterated, "The fundamental point must be that the material force of arms be replaced by the moral force of law. Therefore, a just agreement of all in the simultaneous and reciprocal reduction of armaments according to norms and guarantees to be established, in the measure necessary and sufficient to

maintain public order in the single States; and, as a substitute for arms, the institution of arbitration with its high
pacifying function, according to the norms to be agreed
upon and the sanction to be agreed upon against the State
that refuses either to submit international questions to the
arbitrator or to accept his decision."

We know how it ended and how at the conclusion of
peace the humiliation of Germany favored the birth of
Nazism.

It is interesting to note the red thread that also unites
individuals in the Magisterium of Peace. Eugenio Pacelli,
the future Pius XII, who in 1917 also contributed to the
drafting of Benedict's letter, went on to be consecrated
bishop and sent as Apostolic Nuncio to Munich. On
August 24, 1939, on the eve of the outbreak of World War
II, having now become pope, Pacelli made an unheeded
appeal to stop the conflict unleashed by Hitler and uttered
the following words: "Nothing is lost with peace. All can
be lost with war." The draft of that speech had been prepared by none other than Monsignor Giovanni Battista
Montini, at that time Substitute for the Secretariat of
State, and later Pope Paul VI.

Pius XII's Magisterium of Peace, during the dark years
of the war and in the immediate postwar period, was dedicated to the reconstruction and promotion of a system of
international relations based on dialogue and not on the
use of violence.

His successor, John XXIII, elected in October 1958,
found himself living through the Soviet missile crisis in

Cuba in 1962, with the risk of a nuclear conflict. On October 25 of that year, Pope Roncalli addressed the whole world and its powerful leaders, saying, "Let all those who have responsibilities of power, with their hands on their consciences, listen to the cry of anguish ... from the innocent children to the elderly, from individuals to communities, which rises to heaven: Peace! Peace! I implore all rulers not to remain insensitive to this cry of humanity! Let them do everything in their power to save Peace. . . . Let them promote, encourage, and accept negotiations at every level and at every time!"

And on April 11, 1963, less than two months before his death, John XXIII published the encyclical *Pacem in Terris*, the first by a pontiff dedicated to world peace. He wrote that "human beings live under the nightmare of a hurricane that could break out at any moment with unimaginable force. Since the weapons are there, and if it is difficult to persuade ourselves that there are people capable of taking responsibility for the destruction and pain that a war would cause, it is not excluded that an unpredictable and uncontrollable event could set off the spark that could set the war apparatus in motion."

Pope John also stated, "Justice, wisdom, and humanity demand that the arms race be stopped, that the arms already in existence be simultaneously and reciprocally reduced, that nuclear weapons be banned, and that disarmament, integrated with effective controls, finally be carried out." And quoting verbatim the words of his predecessor Pius XII, he writes, "The calamity of a world war with its economic and social ruins and aberrations and disturbances must not be allowed to overrun humanity for a third time."

John XXIII also reiterated the importance of the United Nations: "We hope, therefore, that the United Nations Organization—in its structures and resources—will be increasingly adapted to the vastness and nobility of its tasks; and that the day will come when individual human beings will find in it effective protection with regard to the rights which flow immediately from their dignity as persons, and that are therefore universal, inviolable, inalienable rights."

His successor Paul VI, before the General Assembly of the United Nations, on October 4, 1965, pronounced his famous cry against war, quoting John Kennedy: "You are waiting for this word from us, which cannot be deprived of gravity and solemnity: not one against the other, not any more, not ever! The United Nations Organization was founded primarily for this purpose; against war and for peace! Listen to the clear words of the great deceased John Kennedy, who four years ago proclaimed, 'Humanity must put an end to war, or war will put an end to humanity.' Not many words are needed to proclaim this supreme goal of this institution. It is enough to remember that the blood of millions of men and countless unprecedented sufferings have been shed, useless slaughters and formidable ruins sanction the pact that unites you with an oath that must change the future history of the world: No more war, no more war! Peace, peace must guide the destiny of peoples and of all humanity!"

In addition to emphasizing continuity, a slow but unstoppable progression should also be noted. This has led the bishops of Rome to intervene more and more, to appeal to international law and to consider as indispensable the role of the United Nations. John Paul II, elected in October 1978, in fact manifests a rejection of war that is even more radical and deep-rooted than his predecessors. And it is interesting to note that Pope Wojtyła's even more decisive and radical rejection of war does not derive only from considerations of principle, but rather from his own experience as a survivor of the catastrophe of the Second World War. He explained this himself, many times, even improvising on the last occasion, at the Angelus of March 16, 2003, when he told "young" rulers of the fate of the world, namely Saddam Hussein, George Bush, and Tony Blair, "I belong to the generation that remembers the war well, that has lived through and, thank God, survived the Second World War. That is why I also have the moral duty to remind the younger ones who do not have this experience. I have a duty to remember and to say: never again war."

In fact, none of his predecessors in the twentieth century knew the horrors of war so directly and so closely as the then-twenty-year-old Karol Wojtyła in Nazi-occupied Poland, one of the countries that paid the highest price, only to come under the influence of the Soviet Union.

From the Falklands conflict to the forgotten wars in Africa, from Lebanon to the Holy Land, from the Gulf War to the crisis in the former Yugoslavia, to Kosovo and

the most recent war in Iraq: John Paul II always inter-
vened personally, utilizing Vatican diplomacy to try to
avoid conflicts and then, once they had broken out, to
propose mediation initiatives and to limit the consequences for the civilian population. The pope strongly
supported multilateralism and the irreplaceable role of the
United Nations. At the same time, he made ecumenism
and dialogue with other religions one of the salient fea-
tures of his pontificate, emphasizing the importance of
the commitment of religions to peace, decades before the
tragic events of September 11, 2001, demonstrated the
urgency of this appeal. The role of the pontiff was decisive in making sure that a large part of the Islamic world
did not experience the subsequent war as a "crusade" and
did not identify the West with Christianity. After the terrorist attacks against the United States, he gathered religious leaders again in Assisi, doing everything possible to
mobilize religious opposition to the abuse of God's name
to justify terrorism, violence, and wars. As the first pope
to enter a mosque, in Damascus, in May 2001, Karol
Wojtyła stressed that "there is no peace without justice
and there is no justice without forgiveness."

This line did not change under Benedict XVI, who,
on the hundredth anniversary of the note of peace of his
predecessor, with whom he shares the same name, said,
"War, with its trail of grief and destruction, has always
been rightly considered a calamity that contrasts with the
plan of God, who created everything for existence and, in
particular, wants to make the human race a family." And

he continued the "purification of memory" begun during the Jubilee Year 2000 by Pope Wojtyła, recognizing, in Assisi, in October 2011, "As a Christian I want to say at this point: yes, it is true, in the course of history, force has also been used in the name of the Christian faith. We acknowledge it with great shame. But it is utterly clear that this was an abuse of the Christian faith, one that evidently contradicts its true nature. The God in whom we Christians believe is the Creator and Father of all, and from him all people are brothers and sisters and form one single family. For us the Cross of Christ is the sign of the God who put 'suffering-with' (compassion) and 'loving-with' in place of force."

The unequivocal choice to say "no to war," which had already cost his predecessors in some crucial occasions various attempts at retrenchment, even within the Church, has continued with even greater decision by Francis. As emerges from the pages of this book, which gathers together the words he has spoken on this theme throughout the first nine years of his pontificate, Pope Bergoglio has warned from the beginning against the risk of a Third World War—a war that he sees as already underway, albeit "in pieces." But these "pieces" are becoming larger and larger, more and more united, and with the outbreak of the conflict caused by the Russian invasion of Ukraine, more and more threatening to the very existence of humanity. For this reason, Francis never tires of discouraging the use of weapons, appealing to everyone. For this reason he asks that hundreds of billions not be spent on increasingly sophisticated weapons, when there are no resources for families, to ensure care, for work, for shelter, and to fight poverty and hunger.

Francis's no to war, a radical and convinced no, like the one pronounced by his predecessors, has nothing to do with a partisan position nor is it motivated by political-diplomatic calculations. In the war in Ukraine there are the aggressors and there are the attacked. There are those who attacked and invaded, killing unarmed civilians, hypocritically disguising the conflict under the guise of a "special military operation"; and there are those who defend themselves by fighting for their land. Francis has said this several times in very clear words, condemning the invasion and martyrdom of Ukraine. This does not mean, however, that he "blesses" the acceleration of the arms race, because the pope is not the "chaplain of the West" and because he reiterates that today being on the right side of history means being against war and seeking peace without leaving any stone unturned. Of course, the *Catechism of the Catholic Church* contemplates the right to self-defense. It does, however, impose conditions, specifying that recourse to arms must not cause evils and disorders more serious than the evil to be eliminated, and remembering that in the evaluation of this consideration, a great weight must be given to the "power of modern means of destruction." Who can deny that humanity is today on the brink of the abyss precisely because of the escalation of conflict and the power of the "modern means of destruction"?

"War," Pope Francis said at the Angelus on Sunday, March 27, 2022, "cannot be something inevitable: we must not get used to war! Instead, we must convert today's outrage into tomorrow's commitment. Because, if we come out of this affair as we did before, we will all be guilty in some way. Faced with the danger of self-destruction, let humanity understand that the time has come to abolish war, to erase it from human history before it erases man from history."